Library Project Funding

CHANDOS
INFORMATION PROFESSIONAL SERIES

Series Editor: Ruth Rikowski
(email: Rikowskigr@aol.com)

Chandos' new series of books are aimed at the busy information professional. They have been specially commissioned to provide the reader with an authoritative view of current thinking. They are designed to provide easy-to-read and (most importantly) practical coverage of topics that are of interest to librarians and other information professionals. If you would like a full listing of current and forthcoming titles, please visit our web site **www.chandospublishing.com** or contact Hannah Grace-Williams on email info@chandospublishing.com or telephone number +44 (0) 1993 848726.

New authors: we are always pleased to receive ideas for new titles; if you would like to write a book for Chandos, please contact Dr Glyn Jones on email gjones@chandospublishing.com or telephone number +44 (0) 1993 848726.

Bulk orders: some organisations buy a number of copies of our books. If you are interested in doing this, we would be pleased to discuss a discount. Please contact Hannah Grace-Williams on email info@chandospublishing.com or telephone number +44 (0) 1993 848726.

Library Project Funding

A guide to planning and writing proposals

JULIE CARPENTER

Chandos Publishing
Oxford · England

Chandos Publishing (Oxford) Limited
TBAC Business Centre
Avenue 4
Station Lane
Witney
Oxford OX28 4BN
UK
Tel: +44 (0) 1993 848726 Fax: +44 (0) 1865 884448
Email: info@chandospublishing.com
www.chandospublishing.com

First published in Great Britain in 2008

ISBN:
978 1 84334 380 6 (paperback)
978 1 84334 381 3 (hardback)
1 84334 380 0 (paperback)
1 84334 381 9 (hardback)

© J. Carpenter, 2008

British Library Cataloguing-in-Publication Data.
A catalogue record for this book is available from the British Library.

Typeset by Domex e-Data Pvt. Ltd.
Printed in the UK and USA.

Contents

Acknowledgements

Many people have unwittingly contributed to this book, not least the authors of the books, published articles and website materials that I have drawn upon and sometimes quote directly, all of whom I have included in my references. I have found their work immensely helpful over the years and I hope that this book builds appropriately on their ideas and expertise.

I am very indebted to my colleagues and friends in Education for Change Ltd, since I have used many examples from project proposals and plans that we have collaboratively drafted, written and submitted for funding, sometimes successfully and sometimes not! In many ways this book is as much the product of their experience as it is of mine.

Julie Carpenter

List of figures and tables

Figures

Tables

List of abbreviations

AHRC	Arts and Humanities Research Council
BL	British Library
CGfL	Community Grid for Learning
CPA/M	critical path analysis/method
DCMS	Department for Culture, Media and Sport
DELOS	Network of Excellence on Digital Libraries
DfES	Department for Education and Skills
DFID	Department for International Development
DP	development partnership
DSC	Directory for Social Change
EfC	Education for Change Ltd
EOI	expression of interest
EPSS	Electronic Proposal Submission Service
ERC	European Research Council
ERPANET	Electronic Resource Preservation and Access Network
ESF	European Social Fund
ESRC	Economic and Social Research Council
EU	European Union
EUCLID	European and International Information, Research and Consultancy Services
EUMEDIS	European Mediterranean Information Society
FP	Framework Programme
HEFC	Higher Education Funding Council
HEI	higher education institute

ICT	information and communications technology
IT	information technology
ITT	invitation to tender
JANET	(formerly) Joint Academic Network
JISC	Joint Information Systems Committee of the HEFC
MGC	Museum and Galleries Commission
MLA	Museums, Libraries and Archives Council
MS	Microsoft
NDPB	non-departmental public body
NESTA	National Endowment for Science, Technology and the Arts
NOF	New Opportunities Fund
OOPP	objective oriented project planning
PC	personal computer
PERT	programme evaluation and review technique
PPM	project planning matrix
PRISM	PReservation of Industrial and Scientific Material
SMART	specific, measurable, acceptable, realistic, time-bound
SME	small and medium-sized enterprise
SWOT	strengths, weaknesses, opportunities, threats
TOR	terms of reference
UNESCO	United Nations Educational, Scientific and Cultural Organisation
UNIDO	United Nations Industrial Development Organisation
USP	unique selling point

About the author

Julie Carpenter is a qualified librarian who began her professional career in the Centre for Learning Resources in the Inner London Education Authority. She joined the British Council in 1978 and travelled widely in Africa, working to improve the Council's own library and information services and managing British book aid programmes. Between 1980 and 1986 she was the Council's Librarian and Assistant Director in Greece. On her return to London Julie took up the new post of Information and Books Projects Officer, collaborating on policy and projects with the Department for International Development (DFID), the World Bank and other development agencies.

Julie has been a consultant since 1990 when she set up Carpenter Davies Associates, a partnership that was successful in developing and managing research projects under the European Union's early R&D Framework Programmes, and working extensively with UK organisations such as the British Library and the Library and Information Commission on strategic research benefiting the library and information communities in a time of considerable change.

She is now a Director of Education for Change Ltd, and has directed and managed a wide range of consulting and research projects focusing on the management of change and the impact of electronic information and digitisation of collections in the education and cultural heritage sectors. She has led research and consulting projects for the

Joint Information Systems Committee (JISC) of the Higher Education Funding Councils, the Museums, Libraries and Archives Council (MLA), the Big Lottery Fund, and several national museums and universities. Her project experience overseas is also broad having worked for DFID, UNESCO, UNIDO, the Asian Development Bank (ADB) and in Central and Eastern Europe, Africa, Asia and the Caribbean.

The author may be contacted at:

j.carpenter@efc.co.uk

Introduction

The increasing 'projectisation' of activities has been a common feature in publicly funded services in recent years, and libraries are no exception. Most library and information services are part of a parent organisation – typically a university or college or local government authority – and their main source of funding has traditionally been a grant or budget allocation from that organisation, with supplementary funds perhaps coming from income-generating activities. Now, however, library and information services are increasingly funded from multiple sources, often reflecting diversification of income at the organisational level, with a greater emphasis on income generation.

This change in funding structures is one factor behind the rise of the project in libraries; a second factor is the widespread adoption of strategic management practices – particularly among academic libraries – requiring strategic planning and action plans, which comprise a combination of projects (a 'programme') directed towards a common purpose, such as change or development in specific areas.

A wide range of opportunities now exists for librarians and other professionals in the cultural heritage sector to obtain external funding for specific project initiatives, or to become involved in research and development projects. Increasingly, service managers respond to new situations using project-based approaches, and government policies are translated into practice through time-limited change programmes, such as Framework for the Future,[1] requiring library organisations to put forward project proposals for funding.

The focus in this book is on planning library projects for external funding rather than project activities that are part of strategic development programmes. However, the principles, advice and tools may also be used in developing good project ideas for internal funding. Many good ideas go to waste simply because the people who have them are not able to persuade key decision-makers of their worth. The ability to turn an idea into a good project proposal is nowadays an essential attribute for both library and information service managers and many staff that report to them.

What is a 'project'?

So what do we mean by a 'project'? Most definitions emphasise the following common features of projects:

- They are temporary – that is, they have definite start and end dates.
- They have definable purposes which almost always involve something unique, some innovation, with results that are different from other day-to-day functions or outputs of the organisation.
- They are planned, managed and resourced separately from, and usually in addition to, normal operations.

Sheila Corrall[2] defines three broad types of project:

- *Runners* – 'bread and butter' undertakings that occur quite frequently and rarely present major challenges as the organisation is well set up to deal with them.

2

- *Repeaters* – 'out-of-the-ordinary' undertakings that happen less often and represent enough variation to require significantly more attention.
- *Strangers* – 'one-off' undertakings, where the organisation has little or no past experience, involving many interests and functions.

She notes that:

> Individual projects are often relatively low-risk undertakings in themselves, but interdependent objectives, shared resources and other demands on staff time increase the risks, making management of project interfaces a key issue. A prime reason for project failure is inadequate priority for resources alongside other projects and day-to-day operations.

External funding

External funding opportunities come in all shapes and sizes, but almost all require some form of bidding procedure, familiar to most commercial sector organisations, for which the proposal development processes differ in scale but not in their nature. Library service managers have traditionally been on the 'client' side of the process, managing public tenders for library automation projects, stock procurement or consultancy contracts. This experience has not necessarily equipped them for responding themselves to tenders and applying for grants. Moreover, other library staff members at all levels are now engaged in developing ideas for projects and identifying potential funding opportunities, and many lack skills and experience in, for instance, strategic planning or resource planning, that would help them achieve successful outcomes.

External funding opportunities, whatever their size, can be grouped into three broad categories which have some common features, and for all of which a similar set of principles and procedures can be applied:

- grant applications;
- calls for proposals;
- invitations to tender (ITTs).

Grant applications

Grant applications are usually associated with charitable foundations and trusts, although librarians and other professionals in cultural heritage will be more familiar with organisations disbursing National Lottery funds in the form of grants, such as the Heritage Lottery Fund and the Big Lottery Fund. Grants may cover all or a portion of project costs; matched funding may be required.

Typically, grant-making organisations will provide broad guidelines on their strategic or priority funding areas and grant-making criteria, or open a particular stream of funding for a limited period, leaving the applicant to interpret their specific project idea within this context. Applications can usually be made at any time, though funders will have their own assessment and funding cycles.

There is great diversity in application procedures among grant-making organisations, ranging from simple presentations of project ideas to more detailed and prescriptive application procedures.

Calls for proposals

Calls for proposals are usually associated with research and development grants, funded, for instance, by the UK

Research Councils or under the European Commission Framework programmes, although charitable trusts and foundations may also use calls as mechanisms to invite proposals for specific funding streams. Calls are time-limited and proposals submitted must conform to specified and often quite prescriptive action lines and priorities. Typically there is a two–three month period between publication of a call and the final submission deadline.

Invitations to tender

Invitations to tender (ITT) can be associated with both research opportunities and service or development contracts. They may be publicly advertised or 'restricted', that is sent to a limited number of pre-selected organisations. Pre-selection may be achieved by inviting preliminary expressions of interest (EOI). ITTs always provide some terms of reference which define the scope and nature of the required inputs and/or outcomes.

How this book can help

This book provides guidelines and tools to help you prepare successful project proposals in response to these kinds of funding opportunities. The actual writing of the successful proposal – a useful skill in itself – is, however, the final stage of what should be a detailed project planning process. Getting the details right is equally as important as writing an attractive proposal. Assembling persuasive evidence based on needs analysis or market research will convince funders more effectively than elegant prose; setting realistic resource and time parameters for your project will make it deliverable in practice as well as feasible on paper. The following chapters will help you through the whole process, from project definition to final proposal preparation.

Identifying and testing the project idea

Chapter 2 describes some essential steps in developing a good project idea, whether in response to a specific funding opportunity or as a consequence of strategic development planning. It considers what kinds of activities are appropriate for project-based approaches and how to ensure a project idea is developed in line with other strategic priorities, and covers issues such as using problem-solving techniques to clarify objectives and stakeholder mapping to identify potential partners.

Matching project ideas and funding opportunities

Chapter 3 addresses practical ways in which good project ideas can be developed to meet the requirements of both the funding organisation and the potential recipient of project funds. It considers a range of external funding organisations in the libraries, information and wider cultural heritage sector, describing their strategic priorities and procedural approaches to project funding.

Building partnerships

Increasingly, a requirement for externally funded projects is collaboration between a diverse range of partner organisations, intended to stimulate cross-sectoral (and, in the case of European Commission funding, cross-border) cooperation and maximise the impact and effectiveness of project outcomes. Working with external partners can complicate both project planning and implementation. Chapter 4 considers how to identify and build effective partnerships.

Assembling evidence

Most external funding organisations require a project rationale supported by some evidence that investment will be justified. Chapter 5 considers what kind of evidence might be needed and how it can be assembled, in particular evidence of appropriate needs or demand among target user groups or other project beneficiaries.

Setting project aims, objectives and outcomes

Coherent aims, objectives and anticipated outcomes are the backbone of every project. Funders are likely to measure your progress and achievements by them, so the importance of getting these right cannot be overstated. Chapter 6 provides practical guidelines on setting realistic and achievable project objectives and outcomes.

Planning the project

Successful project implementation depends upon effective project planning – the identification of resources, scheduling and assigning roles to project participants. Chapter 7 covers the main principles and provides guidelines and checklists.

Using project planning techniques and tools

Chapter 8 identifies some useful tools and applications for project planning and management, and assesses their pros and cons for different kinds of projects.

Monitoring, evaluation and impact assessment

The importance of effective monitoring and evaluation of project progress and outcomes is now widely recognised, and funding organisations will normally expect to see resources dedicated to these tasks, as well as some assessment of potential project impact written into the project proposal. Chapter 9 considers appropriate and practical methodologies.

Writing persuasive proposals

Finally, your work on gathering evidence, developing potential partnerships and planning your project needs to be distilled into a succinct and persuasive proposal that meets the requirements of the funding organisation. Chapter 10 offers advice on techniques and provides some practical examples.

Notes and references

1. *www.culture.gov.uk/Reference_library/Publications/archive_2003/framework_future.htm*
2. Sheila Corrall (2000) *Strategic Management of Information Services: A Planning Handbook*. London: Aslib/IMI.

Defining and testing the project idea

Introduction

The starting point of any project is the moment someone says 'wouldn't it be a good idea if ...', and the process of project definition begins. Maybe this has arisen as a result of a perceived problem or opportunity. In turning the idea into a defined project you will first need to analyse the problem or circumstances carefully and then establish *what you want to achieve*. You then need to consider whether your idea offers the best solution or way forward: are there alternatives which might be equally effective if less attractive? With a clear idea of the direction you want to take, you then need to establish a rough idea of the *costs and resources involved*, an indication of *how much time will be needed* from start to finish and a *way of getting the work done*. Project definition is about discovery and finding common ground and should be time well spent, resulting in a project definition document or project outline that records the decisions taken and identifies the next steps.

Is it really a project?

By their very nature projects are bound to be 'strategic' rather than 'operational' – they are about changing something, introducing a new thing, doing something in a new or different way, the consequences of which for and the impact of which on operations and stakeholders cannot entirely be known or predicted. This 'out of the ordinary' aspect can make projects seem both very attractive and quite risky.

Before you get too far into turning your idea into a project it's a good idea to take a step back and test the basic idea against the key features of projects:

- Is the idea best suited to a temporary and finite set of activities with definite start and end dates? Or would it make more sense to plan and manage it as an integrated part of normal operations?

- Does your idea involve something unique, some innovation, with potential results that are different from other day-to-day functions or outputs of the organisation?

- Is your idea part of a change or development programme? If so, how does it fit or interrelate with other likely or planned projects in the programme? Could your idea be delivered through existing initiatives rather than as an alternative or stand-alone project?

- Do you think your idea could be made to transfer into practice effectively on project completion? If a project is not developed within a strategic planning context there may be difficulties in transferring the outcomes and sustaining the activity in normal operations.

Example: Belfast Exposed NOF Digitisation Programme – definition phase

Belfast Exposed is a dedicated photography gallery that houses an exhibition of contemporary photography, digital archive browsing facilities, a B&W photographic darkroom

---

and an eight-person Apple Mac digital suite. Belfast Exposed has traditionally focused on the development and exhibition of community photography, for which the driving force is the production of socially and politically engaged work and dialogue. Through training it continues to encourage local communities to use photography to record and understand their environment. It was established in 1983 as a radical, politicised community arts organisation, identified closely with the nationalist communities of West Belfast. In the early 1990s, Belfast Exposed became a revenue client of the Arts Council of Northern Ireland and Belfast City Council, and began its community photography educational project.

The question of how best to preserve and open up access to its community photography archive, produced through its activities and accumulated since 1983, became a central preoccupation from 2000. The archive had not hitherto been formally managed or classified and there was little accompanying information with the photographs. Nonetheless, it became clear that the archive had a legitimate role at the heart of the organisation in any future development. Its status as a body of images posed, and continues to pose, important questions about the history of Belfast Exposed, the institutional context of the archive's production, its relationship to the public and, fundamentally, its purpose. The archive has become, for example, the focus of debate around what is community and Belfast Exposed's relationships with its community, making connections between the outreach work and the gallery.

Preservation was the original driver for the definition of a project for possible funding under the NOF Digitisation Programme, but, in fact, working with the archive and defining the project objectives and outcomes began to shape the direction of the organisation in other, more fundamental ways, and change the nature of the planned project into one in which the emphasis was more on access and interpretation from the different users' perspectives.

Getting help to develop your idea

Project definition is not usually something you can do alone, just by fleshing out your original idea. Unless your idea is very simple, straightforward and relatively risk-free, turning it into a potentially viable project proposal is likely to need a group approach. Brainstorming your preliminary idea within a group meeting or more formal workshop is a good way of identifying the potential scope of a project: dependencies will become clearer as will gaps in knowledge or evidence. If you are an enthusiast for mind mapping,[1] a brainstorming session could usefully be aimed at developing a preliminary mind map of the project idea and connected issues and questions.

Below is a checklist to help you decide whether to bring in other people at this stage. The more questions to which you answer 'yes' the more appropriate it is to use group approaches.

Checklist: Should I consult others at this stage?

- Can the problem or opportunity behind your project idea be defined in many different ways?
- To develop the idea, is information from many different sources required?
- Does your idea involve particular specialisation or expertise, where the 'expert' might be biased or not see the wider implications?
- Does the idea have implications for many people?
- Are there likely to be several possible solutions or ways of taking the idea forward?
- Is it a potentially complex idea with many different aspects?
- Will potential activities or solutions need to be agreed by others before it can be implemented?

Assemble a project definition group and some kind of structure or forum for consultation with other colleagues to develop your idea. The group need not include all the people who might eventually work on the project, but should include managers and key staff members in areas where the project is likely to have impact.

Getting key staff involved early on in discussing and considering the project idea has many benefits. Ideally, every member of staff in your organisation whose work might be affected by the potential project should have an opportunity to contribute their views. They will often have a different perspective on the idea and its implications. Even if they cannot directly contribute solutions, what they say may trigger new lines of thought for you: discussion is a great ideas generation technique. Working as a group can also result in more commitment to ideas. Staff should end up feeling a sense of ownership of and commitment to the resulting proposal. Your project idea may be integrated into a wider strategic plan or change programme, and everyone who has been involved in strategic planning exercises knows the value of early and effective communication with staff.

You might also consider including in these preliminary consultations an external adviser with relevant experience, such as a contact who has been involved in similar projects in the past. This kind of advice and valuable recent experience is likely to be particularly beneficial if you are developing project ideas around the use of information and communication technology (ICT) applications, where technology change and know-how can be important factors. The evaluation of the New Opportunities Fund (NOF) Digitisation of Learning Materials Programme,[2] for instance, found low levels of awareness among project organisations about what other projects in the Programme

13

(outside of their immediate region or consortium) were attempting to do or had achieved. Many organisations and individuals that participated in the Digitisation Programme reached a stage where they were able to reflect constructively on how they might better exploit and develop the project outcomes, and to identify with much greater certainty what project planning issues needed addressing, what skills or expertise they required and what technical solutions were indicated.

Using problem-solving approaches

It can be helpful in these early project definition stages to apply 'problem-solving' approaches. Michael Stevens[3] says that problems can be divided broadly into two groups. Maintenance problems exist where the current situation is not as it should be, either because of something failing to happen as expected, or something happening that should not have, i.e. there is a deviation from the 'norm'. The second and more interesting group in this context is achievement problems, where the current situation could be better but there are reasons why it is not, and where an opportunity may exist, for example, to create a new product or service to achieve change.

Analysing a problem involves collecting all relevant information and representing it in a meaningful way, so that, for example, relationships between information can be seen. With achievement problems you will be looking for information which will help to suggest a range of ways to achieve the objective. This analysis also helps you decide what the ideal solution would be, which helps guide your search for practical ways forward. Stevens provides a useful checklist for problem analysis, adapted below to help you define the scope and nature of your objectives in relation to a particular problem.

Checklist: Analysing an achievement problem

- Can this objective (aim or goal) be divided into several sub-objectives?
- Is this objective the ultimate goal in solving the problem or is achieving this objective simply a route to achieving another objective?
- Are there other related objectives?
- What obstacles might prevent you reaching the objective?
- Are there other related obstacles?
- Does this definition of objectives and obstacles take account of the needs of others who are involved or who may be affected?

Preliminary research and information seeking

Finding potential sources of advice and experience is a good reason for undertaking some preliminary research around your initial idea. Research may also:

- reveal whether projects similar in scope and purpose to your idea have been implemented or planned before, and by whom;

- provide you with some indications of potential funding organisations interested in the broad area of your idea;

- lead you to useful and important background documents and material that may help you to define your idea more closely.

External sources of information on ICT-based projects

AHDS-DISCUSS[4] is an open list for projects involved in digitisation. It helps members to locate projects working with practices and standards similar to their own, to identify existing tools and software that can be shared between projects, to get feedback on hardware and software used in data capture, and to provide advice on getting round particular problems.

ProjectsETC[5] is 'an online ideas store' launched by the Department for Culture, Media and Sport (DCMS) Culture Online initiative. The site is intended to help cultural websites 'stand out from the crowd' by encouraging information sharing between institutions and focusing on the overlapping areas of education, technology and culture.

The European Commission Learning and Cultural Heritage Unit provides, at its DigiCULT website,[6] a list of projects funded under the European R&D Sixth Framework Programme (2001–6) and the research areas that were covered relevant to libraries and cultural heritage in general.

Internal information

You will also undoubtedly need to assemble some internal information to help develop and support your project idea. Hard evidence and data will be needed as the basis for developing effective project ideas. It is important to distinguish between facts, ideas, needs and opinions, and to identify early on what information is already available and what will need to be researched or prepared (see checklist below).

Checklist: What information do we need to progress this project idea?

- What kind of information is required (e.g. financial, technical, policy)?
- What specific information is required?
- Why is this information required?
- What are the sources of this information?
- What form will it take?
- How accurate or reliable are the sources?
- How can this information be obtained?

What is this project going to achieve?

In defining a project idea, it is essential that, at the end of the consultation and discussion process, everyone involved is in agreement on and understands exactly what the scope of the project will be – what it will and will not deliver – and what this will mean in broad terms to different strategic and operational agendas within your organisation. If, for instance, the project is to be focused on the work of one department initially, to prepare some intermediate deliverables before extending to other areas or entering another phase, then everyone should be aware of the restricted scope. Similarly, if the project specifically excludes some aspect of work then everyone should be aware of this and why. Of course, the project can be extended to include other tasks as it progresses, if resources and time allow, but the priorities are clear from the start – those objectives that are within the scope of the project take precedence, and everything else is secondary and conditional. Lack of clarity in defining precisely the scope of the project inevitably leads to problems during implementation. Liz MacLachlan[7] includes the following useful example, showing the importance of clarity in defining scope to avoid complexity and 'mission drift'.

Project 3 – Guidance material

In this project the objective is to provide staff electronically with a source of guidance material which is easy to maintain and always up to date. First problem is to define what is meant by 'guidance'. There is a very large amount of material which might be counted as guidance – manuals, notices, desk instructions, books, diagrams and databases. Each of these is different in form and layout. To tackle all of these at once would make a very complex project. The scope needs to be defined very clearly. For example, low-maintenance guidance that does not change much, such as terms of employment, could be left in hard copy but volatile information such as the telephone directory included. Guidance that only a few people see, such as security reports, might be kept on paper but material that everyone is interested in, such as pay scales, computerized.

This does not mean that other material will not be included later on. But with a project like this, which involves a radical change in the way that people work, it makes sense to start with a closely defined set of material and add in others when you are confident that the project will work.

Who is the project for?

Before your project becomes more than an idea you must know who the target beneficiaries are: indeed, the idea is very likely to have arisen from an expressed or perceived audience need. Libraries and archives are increasingly involved in extending their reach within their community, and many projects are likely to address directly the interests of hard-to-reach groups, or are intended to extend access to content and services among excluded communities. These may not be the people that generally walk through the library doors or normally turn to the library for help. For many public and academic libraries, working in partnership with other public services or voluntary sector organisations is the best way to reach and understand these potential target groups. Chapter 5 deals in more detail with assembling evidence of target beneficiary needs, but to define a project you need at least to have a broad view of likely needs, to be able to identify what kind of information and evidence might be required to justify your project and whether additional research is going to be necessary.

Who will be involved?

Project definition should result in a clear idea of who the project stakeholders will be. It is evident from many project evaluations that stakeholders' participation is vital to the successful design and implementation of a project, and this is the moment to think about their involvement.

> **A cautionary note from the NOF Digitisation Programme ...**
> There are several examples of digitisation projects in which problems were encountered in collaboration (or lack of it) with other departments in parent organisations. While the project's strategic importance

may have been acknowledged at senior management level, perceptions in operational departments have sometimes been less positive. Projects were often perceived as completely separate and less important initiatives than the core business, despite apparent synergies in, for instance, collections management, digitisation and website development. These attitudes were reinforced by project timescales, reporting and management methods being dictated by the requirements of the Fund and quite different from those of the parent body. Also, where project teams consisted largely of staff contracted in for the duration, project team members lacked contacts and networks within the parent organisation and an understanding of its organisational culture.[8]

The stakeholders are bound to include various internal colleagues and departments that have been involved in the project definition process. Others will also be included depending upon what skills and experience will be needed.

What other reasons exist for bringing in other partners and stakeholders? It is sensible to undertake a 'stakeholder mapping' exercise, thinking as widely as possible about who might have interests in or be able to make a contribution to the delivery and outcomes of the project. Categorise them in a primary, secondary and tertiary hierarchy. It then becomes easy to see how each stakeholder should be involved and when.

- *Primary stakeholders* are those whose interests lie at the heart of the project. They include potential mainstream providers of funds, supplies or services, and target beneficiaries who experience the problem that the project is aiming to solve and are usually users of services.

- *Secondary stakeholders* need to be involved if your project is to achieve its objectives. This group would include potential partners with similar interests and goals, such as statutory agencies, government departments, voluntary groups and private sector organisations. These stakeholders are where you may find active project partners and co-funders.

- *Tertiary stakeholders* may not be too involved at the beginning but may be important in turning a project into operational reality. These will include policy-makers, practitioners and other organisations working with similar client groups. These stakeholders can be an important category; they will help to support the long-term sustainability of a project.

How long will the project take to deliver ...

Timescales and limits are often imposed by the funding body or parent organisation and rarely is the amount of time available for completion of the project a decision of the project team alone. At the project definition stage it is essential to be absolutely realistic about how long it takes to get things done.

... and how much is it likely to cost?

At this early stage it is important to define what will be the main areas of cost – the types and extent of resources needed to deliver the project as defined (e.g. staff costs, space and facilities, equipment) as well as other costs that might be incurred (e.g. travel costs, marketing and promotion). You should be able to arrive at a set of broad cost parameters that will allow you and your organisation to decide whether the project as defined is feasible or affordable, and whether further effort ought to be devoted to detailed planning and proposal writing.

Find your project champion

Senior managers, with wider, strategic views of how the proposed project might fit into longer-term organisational plans and political priorities will ultimately make the decision to proceed or not with funding or supporting the project in a bid for funds. Their continued support during the implementation of the project could be a crucial factor in its successful outcome. The importance of finding an appropriate project champion, capable of elevating the project up the parent organisation's strategic and operational agendas and willing to use their powers to drive the project forward, is reinforced in numerous project evaluations.[9] With your project idea fleshed out and defined, this is the moment to identify a project champion and persuade them of the merits of the project case. This is the first test of the defined project, so think and prepare arguments to win them over, focusing on what you want to do and why, what the benefits will be and for whom, what the likely cost will be and who might pay, how feasible the project realistically is, and what others think about it.

Below is a summary checklist to see whether you have successfully defined your project idea.

Checklist: The effective project idea

The effective project idea will:

- provide an acceptable level of benefits in terms of the objective;
- deal effectively with potential constraints and their causes;
- take account of any constraints on time, space, human resources and materials;
- appear to be cost-effective and affordable;
- involve an acceptable level of risk;
- be acceptable to stakeholders, in particular:
  - those affected by the defined problem and the proposed solution;
  - those who have to agree the solution;
  - those who might provide the necessary resources;
  - those who have to implement the project.

Notes and references

1. A *mind map* is an image-centred diagram used to represent connected ideas, tasks or other items linked to and arranged radially around a central key word or idea. It is used to generate, visualise, structure and classify ideas, and as an aid in organisation, problem-solving and decision-making. There are numerous software packages that guide the development of mind maps: FreeMind is a good example and downloadable at: *http://freemind.sourceforge.net/wiki/index.php/Main_Page*.
2. The Fund's ICT Content Programmes: final evaluation report, March 2006. See: *http://www.biglotteryfund.org.uk/er_eval_ict_final_rep.pdf*.
3. Michael Stevens (1986) *How to Be a Better Problem Solver*. London: Kogan Page for The Industrial Society.
4. *http://www.jiscmail.ac.uk/lists/AHDS-DISCUSS.html*

5. *http://www.projectsetc.org/*

6. *http://cordis.europa.eu/ist/digicult/projects.htm*

7. Liz MacLachlan (1996) *Making Project Management Work for You,* The Successful LIS Professional series, ed. Sheila Pantry. London: Library Association Publishing.

8. From: *http://www.biglotteryfund.org.uk/er_eval_ict_final_rep. pdf.*

9. For example, in the evaluation of the NOF Digitisation Programme, see: *http://www.biglotteryfund.org.uk/er_eval_ict_final_ rep.pdf.*

Matching project ideas to funding opportunities

Introduction

The vexed issue of where to find funding for good project ideas is becoming an almost constant preoccupation, which is all too frequently associated with declining core budgets for libraries, information services, museums and archives in all sectors. External funding is being increasingly sought to support what could be regarded as 'core business', as Tracey Caldwell notes:[1]

> University library budgets are shrinking. Not only has library funding declined as a proportion of overall institutional spend, it has also failed to keep in step with costs, many of them new.
>
> Some library directors are taking an active and creative approach to the shortfall. They are spearheading fundraising and forging partnerships to save money and attract new budget streams. This is an increasingly central part of their role, and those who have been most innovative and active in their fundraising research have been able to attract considerable sums of money to their library.

It seems likely that the heyday of external and government funding for library and information projects (remember the New Opportunities Fund and the early days of the Heritage

Lottery Fund?) may be over and the policy and operational focus seems, in 2007, to have shifted to community engagement and development, with funds available to support community-based and civil society organisations rather than public sector services. The practical reality is that external project funding is harder to find – as I write this the news is full of how the London Olympics appear to be draining National Lottery money away from the community and heritage funds, and government funding of cultural organisations is likely to suffer adversely in relation to sports in the next spending reviews. Accessing external funds requires even greater creativity and 'thinking outside the box'!

This chapter has limited aims and does not attempt to catalogue the full range of possible funding sources. Rather it addresses the kinds of things that need consideration when trying to identify potential sources and provides some guidance on how to decide where your project idea might comfortably fit in the external funding environment and what the likely chances of a successful outcome might be. Examples of different funders and programmes are used to illustrate points but these come with a health warning – government, Lottery and charitable sector funding changes annually according to political shifts, different organisational policies and priorities, or simply because pots of money run out. A published book is not the place to seek a definitive list of current sources and much information here will already be out of date on publication.

Useful sources of information

The starting point might be a trawl through several key sources of consolidated information.

Grants and government funding

A good place to investigate a very wide range of funding organisations operating in the UK in the social sector is the *Directory for Social Change* (DSC)[2] which was set up in 1975 to be an 'internationally recognised independent source of information and support to voluntary and community sectors worldwide'. The DSC publishes the annually printed *Directory of Grant Making Trusts* with the Charities Aid Foundation, and manages three websites offering good databases and profiled information services covering grant-making trusts and company sponsors (for a modest registration fee) and government funding sources (registration free).

Access to government grants (from the Office of the Deputy Prime Minister, the Home Office, the Department for Education and Skills and the Department of Health) for the voluntary and community sector can be researched at *governmentfunding.org.uk*.[3]

The *National Resource Service*'s database of funding opportunities, the Funding Directory,[4] is intended for information, advice and guidance services and offers a guide through the process of finding financial assistance from non-charitable sources. The Funding Directory offers information on over 600 non-charitable funding schemes and providers around the UK. In addition to searching the database, you can use the directory to track application deadlines and get the latest funding news.

The 'fit4funding'[5] website from the *Charities Information Bureau* lists funding sources from government, the Lottery, the European Community, trusts, banks and building societies and high street stores.

The *Funder Finder*[6] is a small charitable organisation that provides advice and information on grants for charities and voluntary organisations and offers free downloads of software on writing effective funding applications and planning effective budgets. There is also a comprehensive advice pack supplying general funding information and more detailed advice and information on individual schemes such as the local heritage initiative and Community Champions fund.

European funding

European funding remains extremely important to UK public sector and civil society organisations. Academic institutions, in particular, have become much better at accessing European Union (EU) research funding and local government authority organisations often benefit, for instance, from European Social Fund (ESF) funding channelled through the UK government (see below).

Many European Communities grant-making programmes, with a focus on culture, education and information and communications technologies, offer opportunities to libraries, museums and archives to secure funding for collaborative project activities. *EUCLID*,[7] 'European and international information, research and consultancy services', provides consolidated information about most EU funds and funding programmes ('structural', 'transnational' and 'third country') with a focus on funding for 'culture'. EUCLID offers other services apart from their web-based information and alerting service, and their seminars and publications about funding for cultural organisations are good places to start if you are unfamiliar with the EU funding landscape.

Examples of funders and programmes of interest to cultural heritage organisations

European Union programmes

If your project idea has, or could have, an international dimension then European funding may be an option. There is a very wide range of funding opportunities among the various EU programmes supporting education, lifelong learning, social inclusion and mobility, research and development, ICT use and innovation and international cooperation. The range is too wide and complex for this book. The European Union EUROPA website has all the details but it is a challenge to navigate successfully around it. I recommend the use of intermediaries such as EUCLID (see above) and others.[8] Below are some brief introductions to programmes worthy of investigation.

European Social Fund Programme 2007–13

The European Social Fund (ESF) programme will contribute to sustainable economic growth and social inclusion by extending employment opportunities and by developing a skilled and adaptable workforce. The managing authority for the ESF programmes in England is the Department for Work and Pensions. In Scotland, Wales and Northern Ireland the managing authorities are the Scottish Executive, the Welsh Assembly Government and the Department for Employment and Learning.

It is expected that the first funding rounds under the 2007–13 programme will be held in autumn 2007 and that project activity will start in early 2008. The ESF spent £578 million on employment and training projects in England in

2006. Spending in 2007 (on continuing activities funded under the 2000–6 programme) is likely to be at a similar or even higher level. The programme contains six priorities (see Table 3.1).

There are two routes for applying for European Social Fund (ESF) support: co-financing and alternative bidding. The vast majority of ESF activity will be funded through the co-financing method. Co-financing brings together ESF and domestic matched funding such as funding from the Learning and Skills Councils or Jobcentre Plus in a single 'pot' to produce a single funding stream. Organisations managing these funds are called co-financing organisations (CFOs). Major CFOs include the Learning and Skills Council and Jobcentre Plus, together with some local authorities, Connexions partnerships and Business Links. Since April 2003, the great majority of ESF funds has been channelled through CFOs. Government office websites give details of the CFOs in each region, together with information on which measures and activities CFOs will be co-financing.

Table 3.1 ESF funding priorities 2007–13

	Regional Competitiveness and Employment Objective All of England and Gibraltar except Cornwall and the Isles of Scilly	Convergence Objective Cornwall and the Isles of Scilly
Worklessness	Priority 1: Extending employment opportunities (€1,794 million ESF)	Priority 4: Tackling barriers to employment (€75 million ESF)
Workforce skills	Priority 2: Developing a skilled and adaptable workforce (€984 million ESF)	Priority 5: Improving the skills of the local workforce (€118 million ESF)
Technical assistance	Priority 3: Technical assistance (€116 million ESF)	Priority 6: Technical assistance (€4 million ESF)

Equal[9]

Equal is an initiative funded through the European Social Fund (ESF). Equal operates across identified thematic fields related to the four pillars of the European Employment Strategy and support for asylum seekers. The programme tests and promotes new means of combating all forms of discrimination and inequalities in the labour market, both for those in work and for those seeking work. Equal also includes action to help the social and vocational integration of asylum seekers.

Equal in Great Britain[10] operates in the following thematic fields:

- employability;
- entrepreneurship;
- adaptability;
- equal opportunities.

In addition to these themes, the programme supports a further theme of activities to help the social and vocational integration of asylum seekers. Throughout those themes the current strategy for Equal in Great Britain aims to:

- ensure that activities principally benefit those subject to the main forms of discrimination and inequality and each thematic field will be fully accessible to all such groups;
- ensure that the promotion of equality between women and men is integral to the thematic fields in all four pillars as well as being targeted through specific actions in the fourth pillar;
- promote the ideal of improving the supply of and demand for quality jobs with a future;
- encourage the effective use of existing mechanisms (for example, those that exist for social dialogue) to improve

awareness of the factors leading to discrimination, inequality and exclusion in connection with the labour market.

Equal funds activities that are implemented by strategic partnerships called development partnerships (DPs), which bring together key actors (local and regional authorities, training bodies, public employment services, NGOs, enterprises, social partners) on a geographical or sectoral level. Equal encourages participation and transnational cooperation.

Two calls for proposals for projects in the member states have taken place so far, the first in 2001 and the second in 2004. Funding from the second round will end in December 2007, after which a third round is expected. The allocation of funds to the UK for Equal has been split between Great Britain, Northern Ireland and Gibraltar. Northern Ireland operates and funds its own programme arrangements except for those for asylum seekers, for which there is one single funding stream covering all of the UK.

EU Lifelong Learning Programme: The Grundtvig Programme[11]

The Grundtvig Programme is part of the European Commission's new Lifelong Learning Programme and aims to strengthen the European dimension in adult education and lifelong learning across Europe. Grundtvig specifically seeks to address the educational challenge of an ageing population and to provide adults with alternative pathways to updating their skills and competences. Grundtvig encompasses all types of learning, whether these take place in the 'formal' or 'non-formal' system of education for adults, or in more 'informal' ways, such as autonomous learning, community learning or experiential learning. Anyone in adult education can participate, including adult learners, teachers and trainers from a variety of organisations including local authorities, non-governmental organisations, charities, universities, community groups, etc.

'Adult' in the Grundtvig sense refers to all persons over the age of 25 and all persons aged 16–24 who are no longer undergoing initial education within the formal education system. Grants are available for a wide range of activities. Some examples are basic skills, foreign languages, parental education, arts and culture. All projects involve working with European partners and offer a great learning and personal development experience for staff and learners.

Any organisation involved in formal, non-formal and informal adult education can apply for a Learning Partnership. This includes a wide variety of organisations, including local authorities, colleges, charities, trade unions, voluntary and community groups, prisons, etc.

EU Research and Innovation Programme[12]

Financial support for research is made available chiefly through calls for proposals which are issued for each specific programme of the Framework Programme (FP7).

FP7 is divided into four programmes. The 'Cooperation' programme will support research cooperation in a number of key thematic areas, addressing specific sectors such as life sciences, information and communication technologies and food quality and safety research. 'Ideas' will fund investigator-driven research through a newly created European Research Council (ERC). The 'People' programme will support training and researchers' career development, while 'Capacities' will fund the coordination and development of research infrastructure, regional research clusters, international cooperation and closer ties between science and society. A 'road map' of the planned calls for proposals can be found in the work programme for each specific programme.

The ICT Work Programme[13] may be of particular interest to libraries. ICT is regarded as critical to improve the competitiveness of European industry and to meet the demands of its society and economy. ICT is considered to have catalytic impact in three key areas:

- productivity and innovation, by facilitating creativity and management;

- modernisation of public services, such as health, education and transport;

- advances in science and technology, by supporting cooperation and access to information.

The Tempus Programme:[14] changes in higher education through people to people cooperation

The Tempus Programme is based on the understanding that higher education institutions are of particular importance for the social and economic transition process as well as cultural development; they are also pools of expertise and human resources and provide for the training of new generations of leaders. Tempus focuses on the development of the higher education systems in the EU accession and neighbouring countries through cooperation with institutions from member states of the EU.

The Tempus Programme reached the end of its third funding round at the end of 2006 and will be continued over the period 2007 to 2013. Once a stand-alone programme, Tempus is now financed through:

- the Instrument for Pre-accession Assistance that covers the Western Balkans;

- the European Neighbourhood and Partnership Instrument that covers countries of Eastern Europe, North Africa and the Middle East; and

- countries from the Central Asian region, which receive assistance from the Development and Cooperation Instrument.

In the past the Tempus Programme has funded cooperation projects in the areas of curriculum development and innovation, teacher training, university management and structural reforms in higher education. It has certainly encompassed both stand-alone university library and information service development projects and enhancement of information services as components of wider projects. It puts special emphasis on the mobility of academic and administrative staff from higher education institutions, both from the EU and the partner countries. Tempus projects are organised as consortia between institutions in EU member states and those in the partner countries. In each EU member state, a National Contact Point[15] offers advice and assistance to prospective and current Tempus projects.

Grant-making bodies in the UK

Apart from direct UK government funding which is not covered here, there are many public and private sector organisations in the UK that provide grants for project-based activities. Relatively few include cultural heritage among their funding priorities, although community development through arts and creative initiatives as well as lifelong learning and social engagement and inclusion are familiar funding objectives. Examples include the following.

The Joint Information Systems Committee (JISC)[16] of the Higher Education Funding Councils (HEFCs)

JISC's mission is 'to provide world-class leadership in the innovative use of Information and Communications Technology to support education and research.' JISC funds a national services portfolio (e.g. the JANET academic network) and a range of programmes (e.g. JISC Capital Programmes, the e-Learning innovation programme) and projects (e.g. independent radio news archive digitisation). Most of these initiatives originate from a successful response to a circular or tender, inviting organisations to bid for funding.

JISC also tenders for contractors among the higher and further education community to undertake specific research studies or provide technical support on its behalf. For example the latest of these tenders at the time of writing (August 2007) is a tender to provide expert support to the Digital Repositories programme and, in particular, to the Common Repositories Interfaces Group. A total of £150,000 is available for this project.

As an indication of the range and scope of JISC funding opportunities Table 3.2 summarises the Capital Programme Call for Projects issued in July 2007. Project proposals are invited from any higher education institution funded by the HEFCs in England and Wales and any further education institution in England that offers higher education courses.

The Arts and Humanities Research Council (AHRC)[17]

The AHRC museum and gallery schemes are open to museums, galleries and special collections located within, or forming part of, higher education institutions that are

Table 3.2	JISC Capital Programme Call for Projects July 2007		

Programme/ initiative	Theme/ context	Description	Funds
Enterprise Architectures	Enterprise Architecture Group Pilot	Projects to investigate an enterprise architecture approach to service oriented development at institutional level through the application and evaluation of The Open Group Architecture Framework (TOGAF)	Total funds: £500,000, c.10 projects, up to £50,000 available per project, 12 months duration
e-Research: e-Infrastructure	Federated Tools and Services	Projects to explore the area of new technologies for control of access to research data	Total funds: £500,000, 1–3 projects, 12–15 months duration
Users and Innovation	Next Generation Technologies and Practices (Phase 2)	(a) Projects to develop and/or adapt next generation technologies and practices, in order to undertake small-scale pilots (b) Projects to develop, adapt and deploy next generation technologies and practices, in order to undertake large-scale institutional demonstrators	Total funds: c.£2,500,000 (a) 10 projects, maximum funding of £50,000 available per project (b) 10 projects; £150,000 to £200,000 available per project; up to 15 months duration

funded directly by the Higher Education Funding Council for England (HEFCE). The AHRC's Project Fund scheme provides awards to support well-defined projects of up to 12 months in duration that will bring about significant improvements in the stewardship of small university-based collections of regional, national or international importance to higher education.

The AHRC is currently (2007) developing a Museums and Galleries Research Programme, an integrated strategy for supporting research in UK museums, galleries, libraries and archives. This programme is distinct from the support for higher education museums, galleries and collections on behalf of the HEFCE in that it is not limited to England or to university museums. The aim is for this programme to operate as an umbrella programme, pulling together existing funding opportunities, offering specific funding for certain activities and supporting other activities of interest to the sector. The programme is currently arranged around four main themes: research project funding; partnerships; people; and impact and evaluation.

The Esmée Fairbairn Foundation[18]

The Esmée Fairbairn Foundation is one of the largest independent grant-making foundations in the UK. They make grants to organisations that aim to improve the quality of life for people and communities in the UK, both now and in the future. They 'like to consider work which others may find hard to fund, perhaps because it breaks new ground, appears too risky, requires core funding, or needs a more unusual form of financial help such as a loan.' The Foundation currently (in 2007) makes grants in four areas:

- Arts and Heritage;
- Environment;
- Education;
- Social Change: enterprise and independence.

The Joseph Rowntree Foundation[19]

The Foundation funds research projects in key social policy areas such as housing, poverty and disadvantage, and neighbourhood renewal. It issues calls for proposals related to specific work programmes throughout the year and will only accept applications for funding in response to these calls.

The Museums, Libraries and Archives Council (MLA)[20]

The MLA, as most readers of this book will already know, is the lead strategic agency for museums, libraries and archives, part of the wider MLA Partnership made up of itself and nine regional agencies. The MLA works in partnership and collaborates with government departments, national and international organisations, and umbrella bodies and other national departmental public bodies (NDPBs) and development agencies. The MLA does make grants to publicly funded organisations in the cultural heritage sector that 'promote different aspects of the work of museums, libraries and archives'. It also manages grant funding within the remit of national programmes, such as the Framework for the Future and Renaissance in the Regions. The eligibility criteria for grant funding differ from scheme to scheme, and at any one time different schemes may be open for applicants.

For example, at the time of writing the PReservation of Industrial and Scientific Material (PRISM) Grant Fund, which awards up to £250,000 each year to museums and other heritage-based organisations in England and Wales, reported that 32 grants totalling £237,000 have been awarded in the past year to help museums to acquire and conserve items of outstanding scientific or industrial importance.

The MLA Partnership also announced the launch of a second phase of the Big Lottery funded Their Past Your Future programme. In this second phase of the programme, which runs from 2007 to 2010, the MLA Partnership will manage an annual grant programme open to all museums, libraries and archives in England. The programme will offer funding for the sector to use their collections to explore innovative and creative ways of increasing community learning and young people's knowledge and understanding of the impact and significance of conflict.

Lottery funding[21]

There are several routes to Lottery funding which might offer opportunities for new partnerships. In the libraries, museum and archives world, however, the Heritage Lottery Fund and the Big Lottery Fund stand out as the principal funders in the sector.

The Heritage Lottery Fund[22]

The Heritage Lottery Fund helps non-profit groups with projects to conserve and enhance the UK's diverse heritage, encourage more people to be involved in their heritage and make sure that everyone can learn about, have access to and enjoy their heritage. The fund currently operates a number of grant schemes, including:

- Your Heritage (grants from £5,000 to £50,000) for projects that increase opportunities for learning about heritage and open up heritage resources and sites to the widest possible audiences. These can include caring for the natural landscape, conserving historic buildings, places and objects, involving people in exploring local cultures, traditions, languages and ways of life;

- Heritage Grants (£50,000 plus), for which projects might include nature conservation, historic buildings, museum collections, archive collections, spoken history records, cultural traditions, and objects and sites relating to the UK's industrial, transport and maritime history.

The Big Lottery Fund[23]

BIG, as the Fund styles itself, is the largest distributor of Lottery money. In 2006–7 they handed out £630 million to community organisations and projects for health, education and the environment. The Fund offers a rather bewildering array of different programmes, with differing emphases, for England, Scotland, Wales and Northern Ireland, as well as an International Grants programme, all of which have varying project funding limits and programme start dates. In the past it has run programmes of direct significance to cultural heritage organisations, such as Community Libraries (2005–6), and the focus on community development and empowerment is unlikely to change radically for a number of years. The current programmes will end in 2008 and a new set of programmes and funding priorities is under discussion at the time of writing.

National Endowment for Science, Technology and the Arts (NESTA)[24]

NESTA is 'the largest single endowment devoted exclusively to supporting talent, innovation and creativity in the UK'. It has endowed funds of over £300 million from the National Lottery and uses the interest from the endowment, the returns from its investments and other public and private sources of income to fund activities. NESTA invests in early-stage companies, informs innovation policy and encourages a culture that helps innovation to flourish.

NESTA is not primarily a grant-making organisation; however, it has a range of programmes that provide financial and non-financial support to individuals and organisations. These are tightly defined and focused on specific topics, and generally involve NESTA issuing a 'call for proposals'.

In March 2007 NESTA launched a new programme called Innovation Challenges, which focuses on 'social innovation'. NESTA expects to fund 'a series of experimental, high-impact projects, designed to create opportunities for innovation in response to major social issues' and sees social innovation as innovation in response to social needs or challenges, generated by organisations, individuals and enterprises whose primary purposes are social and where 'profit' is reinvested. NESTA is interested in innovations in:

- processes and service delivery;
- products;
- technologies.

So how do you decide where to search for project funding?

There are really four fundamental questions to ask with regard to starting the search for project funding.

What type of organisation are you and your partners?

Most funding agencies and programmes have eligibility rules governing the kinds of organisations they will assist with project funding and this should be the first thing you check in your trawl through the possibilities. If yours is a public sector organisation, receiving statutory or other government funding, you may be ineligible to bid for funds from some charitable trusts. In some EU programmes academic institutions are prime targets; in others they are ineligible as project leaders or coordinators. UK research funding councils deal almost exclusively with higher education and research organisations, though other kinds of organisation can be part of a research project proposal. Voluntary and charitable organisations are usually welcome everywhere as project partners but not necessarily as project leaders or coordinators, unless they are over a certain size (in terms of annual turnover). Private sector organisations are ineligible to receive some lottery funds, though they can be included in project partnerships and as subcontractors.

Most funding organisations actively encourage project partnerships which include several different types of organisation, and this can often be a way around the constraints of eligibility rules: the question of which partner leads the project may be determined by which matches best the potential funder's requirements.

What is the broad focus or sector of your project?

Funding organisations and programmes all have priority sector and subject areas in which they wish to focus their support. These may – indeed are very likely to – change over time, with shifts in government policy, the emergence of new social and technological issues, and perceived 'saturation' of funding in particular areas. The Big Lottery Fund is a good example of this kind of priority setting and shift in focus. New funding programmes also emerge – in particular from the European Commission – in response to social and technological change.

The priorities of most funders remain in place for three to five years. Currently four focus areas of interest to libraries, museums and archives can be identified:

- arts and cultural;
- education and training;
- lifelong learning;
- community and social welfare and regeneration.

Figure 3.1 positions the funding organisations we have considered in this chapter in relation to those four focus areas, giving an indication of their current priorities.

Figure 3.1 Funding organisations and their sectors of interest

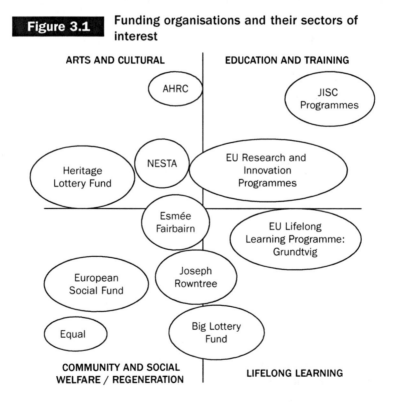

What kind of funding are you looking for?

Different funding organisations will fund different kinds of things, both in terms of the types of inputs, activities and outcomes you are planning and in terms of different types of costs. Without becoming bogged down in detail at this stage, it is important to think broadly about the kind of funding you will need and match this to the interests of potential funders. As a guide, the Directory of Social Change uses the following kinds of categories:

- advocacy;
- building/renovation;
- collection or acquisition;
- computer systems, hardware development funding;
- equipment;
- evaluation;
- full project funding;
- project funding excluding overheads;
- publication;
- replacement or statutory funding;
- research;
- seed funding;
- service delivery;
- strategic planning.

How are your project beneficiaries defined?

As with focus areas and sectors, funding organisations tend to set priorities with regard to the direct or indirect target beneficiaries of projects they will support. While you may define your target audiences and beneficiaries differently to most funding agencies it is important to try to achieve a match between their interests and yours.

The Directory of Social Change uses the following characteristics of project beneficiaries in relation to current funder priorities in the UK.

- age;
- class, group, occupation or past occupation;
- disability;
- ethnicity;
- gender and relationships;
- ill health;
- nationality;
- religion;
- social or economic circumstances.

Notes and references

1. Tracey Caldwell (2006) 'Sing for your supper – how uni libraries win budgets', *Information World Review*, 4 September, at: *http://www.iwr.co.uk/information-world-review/features/2163542/sing-supper-uni-libraries-win*.
2. *http://www.dsc.org.uk/aboutdsc.html*
3. *http://www.governmentfunding.org.uk/Default.aspx*
4. *http://www.advice-resources.co.uk/adviceresources/general/dir/fun_dir/*
5. *http://www.fit4funding.org.uk/*
6. *http://www.funderfinder.org.uk/*
7. *http://www.euclid.info/*
8. *http://www.welcomeurope.com*

9. *http://ec.europa.eu/employment_social/equal/about/index_ en.cfm*
10. For information on Equal in the UK see: *http://www.equal .ecotec.co.uk/.*
11. *http://www.lifelonglearningprogramme.org.uk/how-to-apply .asp*
12. *http://cordis.europa.eu/news/calls_en.html*
13. *http://cordis.europa.eu/fp7/ict/*
14. *http://ec.europa.eu/education/programmes/tempus/index_ en.html*
15. In the UK information from the National Contact Point is at Canterbury University and can be accessed at: *http://www .tempusuk.ac.uk/index.php.*
16. *http://www.jisc.ac.uk*
17. *http://www.ahrc.ac.uk/*
18. *http://www.esmeefairbairn.org.uk/about_us.html*
19. *http://www.jrf.org.uk/default.asp*
20. *http://www.mla.gov.uk*
21. *http://www.lotteryfunding.org.uk*
22. *http://www.hlf.org.uk/English/*
23. *http://www.biglotteryfund.org.uk/*
24. *http://www.nesta.org.uk/index.aspx*

4

Building partnerships

Introduction

A requirement for many externally funded projects is collaboration between a range of different partner organisations, intended to stimulate cross-sectoral (and in the case of European Commission funding, cross-border) cooperation and maximise the impact and effectiveness of project outcomes. This chapter considers how to build effective partnerships. It draws on an excellent sourcebook produced by SQW Ltd for the New Opportunities Fund, and never, as far as I know, formally published. Fortunately it is still available (in 2007) on the Web[1] and I recommend it.

Where not to start!

The best and most successful partnerships are built voluntarily from an early, 'ideas' stage and go through several negotiation phases and iterations before the partnership structure is finalised for project implementation. The worst possible ways to approach partnership working is to start looking for appropriate partners as and when a funding or project opportunity arises, or to 'cobble together' a partnership under pressure to meet specific funder's requirements. However, that has often been the most typical approach adopted:

> It was unrealistic to expect that all the NOF Digitisation Consortia partnerships could miss out these essential and time-consuming partnership-building phases and still work harmoniously under the pressures of programme implementation, and it is all the more remarkable that those consortia that were made to function managed to be so creative. Several consortia also represented the most difficult kind of partnership working: that of partnerships between organisations from very different organisational cultures as well as different domains – for instance, a national museum working with local authority library organisations. There are lessons to be learned here for future programmes related to the need to address organisational and cultural issues directly early in the partnership-building process, and not underestimating the power of bureaucratic and procedural issues to undermine effective partnership working.[2]

While it is tempting to be guided in your search for partners by the requirements of the most likely looking funding organisations (each of which, as the previous chapter shows, have their own policies and priorities when it comes to the kinds of organisation they want to work with), there are better criteria that you should apply, before considering external requirements. First of all let's consider the nature of organisational partnerships.

Example: Reluctant partners! The case of Consortium A

Consortium A was a national partnership developed to fulfil the requirements of the second stage of a Lottery funding application in which the potential partners had been identified by the fund as having project ideas within the same very broad subject area. The potential partners were one national and one large regional cultural organisation and three local authority library services in various regions of England.

After discussions and partner meetings it was decided that Consortium A would be 'a series of largely independent projects, each receiving a grant under an overarching lead partner who has a co-ordinating role including responsibility for identifying any potential areas of duplication (e.g. in materials to be processed)'. This decision reflected:

- ambivalent attitudes towards the consortium approach;
- the desire of local authority partners to retain control over their own budgets;
- reluctance on the part of the national museum (nominated as the lead partner) to commit to a highly centralised structure which was perceived as likely to be complex and labour-intensive to manage.

The consortium partners shared an early awareness of potential difficulties in consortium building and management, arising from, for instance:

- very different IT situations and capacities among the partners;
- different perspectives on strategic goals between the national and local authority organisations;
- diverse project aspirations, subjects and goals.

What does 'partnership' mean?

It would be surprising if your organisation does not already have active working relationships with a number of organisations from the public, private and voluntary sectors. These could be said to be partnerships rather than straightforward customer–supplier relationships if the organisations work together to pursue a common vision and achieve more or different things than any of them could on their own. Effective local partnerships are very common; national and international ones much less so, although you may hear the term 'partnership' used to describe all types of collaboration! Often such partnerships are informal groupings, but where external finance and contracts with third parties are on the agenda, it is certain that the partnership will need to be formalised in some way. If you are about to consider finding new partners in a project initiative, or if you have been approached to join another potential project partnership, you need to think carefully about the benefits, potential costs and risks.

Benefits of partnership working

What will your organisation get out of the partnership?

If your only answer to this question is that it will fulfil the requirement for applying for project funding then you should think again about the whole idea! You must be able to identify some positive and substantive benefits in working with the right partners: for instance, they might bring skills and know-how essential to the project that are lacking within your own organisation; they might have a particular track record or high profile in the field or they might bring a different perspective on the project issues from another sector.

What does your organisation offer to the partnership?

Mutual benefit in the partnership must be clear from the start – beyond the promise of extra funding if the project application is successful. Work out what your organisation's main strengths are and whether they complement those of the kinds of partner you have in mind.

What will be the 'added value' in the partnership?

Partnerships must add up to more than the sum of their parts. Think about how the partnership you have in mind might appear to an external assessor. Will it provide an advantageous geographical reach, or a target workforce capacity? Is the combination of partners likely to be unique or innovatory?

Costs of partnership working

Three different kinds of costs to your organisation that are associated with partnership working need consideration: transaction costs, effort and time, and financial costs.

Transaction costs

These are the costs incurred in the process of setting up the partnership – including researching and negotiating with potential partners, identifying the right partners and possibly rejecting the less appropriate ones. These costs can be minimised if you are considering entering into partnership with organisations that you already know, work with or have worked with in the past, where a level of understanding and communication is already established.

Effort and time

Once partners are identified and on board you should be under no illusions about how much effort and time it will take to run the partnership, whether your organisation is managing it or only involved in some other way. Building relationships takes time. Many successful organisational partnerships have taken years to evolve and develop. Sometimes organisations will have completely different working cultures. If you are going to work with international partners there can also be significant social and cultural differences and the early stages of building a partnership can be quite a bumpy ride! It isn't just the time required for involvement in or organising meetings that you need to take into account here. You need to build into your project planning, for instance, sufficient time for drafting and redrafting documents, for document translation perhaps, and for formal and informal discussion and debate leading to collaborative decision-making.

Financial costs

In addition to the obvious staff costs involved in building and running partnerships, there are always hidden costs involved in partnership working – for instance, travel costs to get to meetings in a regional, national or international partnership, communications costs, training costs and capacity-building costs. These may be hard to anticipate at the start, but should be addressed collaboratively and accurately estimated once the partnership is operational.

Establishing constructive working relationships

In approaching other groups and organisations to establish working relationships, SQW offer three helpful tips that are especially important in the early stages.

Be clear about what you want

Most people are busy. It helps to have a clear idea of what it is that you want from the other organisation. Make sure that you communicate this to them as succinctly as possible.

Speak to the right people

Finding the right person to speak to and to involve in the partnership process is crucial. They should be someone whose remit or job covers the area or issue that you are interested in and who has some influence or seniority in the organisation. It may take several calls or even meetings to find the right person. Face-to-face meetings can help to emphasise your seriousness and build relationships and trust. An informal approach is better at first, before making formal proposals.

Try to understand what they want

It helps to have an understanding of the constraints and priorities of the other organisation. If you are not familiar with them, you may want to do some informal research into what their aims and priorities are. Are you able to offer them some benefits or opportunities? Partnerships should be 'win-win' situations.

> ... **Partnerships are about people,** first and foremost. The most effective partnerships are often those that consist of committed, hard-working people who communicate and work well with each other. The quality of relationships between individuals is crucial. Nowhere is this more important than in the first stages of partnership development when organisations seek to establish new or different arrangements. Always make sure that newcomers and new colleagues are properly introduced and briefed about the partnership and who they will be working with. First impressions count.
>
> ... **Trust and respect** are central to effective partnerships. If the core partners do not regard each other as 'equals' or as reliable partners, it may be very difficult to work together. This can often be a problem for community and voluntary groups trying to work with statutory or private organisations. Organisations that are seeking to work across sectors or with new organisations may find that they have unhelpful 'stereotypical' views of each other.[3]

Ways of working in partnership

The focus here is on the 'setting up' stage of a partnership rather than how partnerships actually deliver. In practice, of course, the development of a partnership may be such that you end up working out internal systems and structures at the same time as actually delivering projects! There are risks in doing this: for example, enthusiasm at new relations and opportunities can disguise intrinsic and fundamental differences. Partners may be reluctant to raise misgivings or problems early on for fear of damaging potential relationships. In the early stages, therefore, it is important for your partnership to address a number of issues associated with developing relationships and mutual understanding, as well as planning actions.

Defining roles and responsibilities

From the start it is important to acknowledge that not all partners will have, or feel that they have, equal weight or power in the decision-making processes. When deciding upon roles and responsibilities, therefore, it will help for all partners to be honest about this issue and take it into account. The final decision on what role each organisation has should be agreed by all partners and should seek to provide for a reasonable balance of power between partners.

Establishing a workable structure

It is likely that your organisation will have had experience of working in partnership with others and will have preferred structures and legal models. They may, however, not be appropriate for a project (i.e. time-limited) partnership. SQW summarises three possible options and the associated pros and cons (see Table 4.1).

Building your capacity to get involved in partnership working

Working in partnership may be a new experience for you or your organisation. Even for those used to it, getting involved

Table 4.1   Partnership structure options

Option	Description	Pros and cons
Company limited by guarantee	Establishes a legal company which is 'not for profit' and which is governed by a memorandum and articles of association. Requires annual accounts to be submitted to Companies House	Offers flexibility Legal status allows the company to employ staff, enter into contracts and make payments Creates an 'independent' organisation which is separate from any particular partner Offers some protection to individuals against personal liability Costs of annual auditing are incurred
Partnership agreement	A legally binding agreement between two or more organisations Can be for any purpose and can take numerous forms (e.g. joint venture)	Appropriate for project-specific or other clearly delineated activities Legally binding agreement
Voluntary association	Organisations agree to cooperate and may define their mutual commitment in a memorandum The partnership has no legal status or recognition	Easy and cheap to establish Flexible and informal Cannot employ staff or enter into contracts, so must rely on a partner organisation to do this on its behalf

in a new initiative or partnership often means meeting new agencies, groups and people. Not all the key people will necessarily have had experience of this type of working; not all may have the same skills or confidence. For some it may involve a change of working culture. So, it may be appropriate to review skills and feelings towards joint working in your organisation and in the other partners, and assess whether any training, relationship building or other work may be helpful. A failure to address such issues may lead to problems arising, with some partners becoming frustrated or others becoming too dominant.

Effective action planning

Any project partnership should have a clear action plan to guide its project delivery. It may cover one year or several. It may alternatively be called a delivery plan or a business plan. The potential funder of your project may have very specific requirements about the structure and contents of the action plan or business plan and any such guidance is worthy of careful scrutiny!

The purpose of an action plan is to define who is going to do what, when, where and how. It should be a practical document and one that all partners will need to sign up to. If you have chosen partners well, it will be closely aligned to the original project plan and is likely, therefore, to contain:

- aims and objectives of the project;
- who the intended beneficiaries are;
- description of the project and strategy;
- who will manage the project;
- timeline and milestones/key events;
- outline project costs and the sources of funding;
- defined outputs and benefits of the project;
- forward strategy;
- evaluation framework.

Example: Management and decision-making in a partnership

Consortium A had been set up as a 'loosely managed partnership' with collaborative management structures based on discussion and consensus, leaving each of the individual projects a high degree of autonomy over their own project implementation schedules, content and approaches. However, web-based projects, by their nature, require a high level of hands-on management, with detailed and timely decisions on, for instance, website design and branding, metadata structures and shared technical approaches to ensure interoperability. A certain amount of tension existed from the start between the partners' idea of how the consortium would work and the real demands of delivering the projects as planned. A rather more autocratic management style than had originally been envisaged was in fact employed in response to the practical need to deliver on detailed operational plans, in which agreement/consent on many critical success factors was very time-sensitive with much less scope than anticipated for discussion, awareness and consensus-building.

Engagement in the consortium management process by all partners was also made more complex by the varied and different policies, priorities and planning structures among project partner organisations; it was not always possible for the individual project managers to make or agree to decisions on behalf of their organisations without referral. For instance, decisions involving ICT systems or tendering processes might have to be referred back to other departments in a local authority for either consultation or endorsement.

In the consortium business plan, the time-consuming nature of partnership management had been underestimated, and all partners underestimated the management time involved in collaborative working and negotiating consortium decisions. Project managers quickly experienced tension between their own project management duties and their contributions to consortium collaboration and management.

Roles and responsibilities: who does what in a partnership

Within most partnerships it is possible to identify similar types of roles that organisations can play. The challenge is to agree which partners should play which roles and agree a workable division of responsibilities. A typical partnership arrangement might have three levels of involvement.

Decision-making

Although decisions should be taken at all levels of partnerships, this is the group or body whose role is to take ultimate responsibility for the partnership and its activities. The tasks of this body – often called the board or management committee – could include:

- agreeing the vision, aims and objectives of the partnership;
- agreeing the constitution/memorandum of association or similar;
- formulating policies and strategies;
- giving final approval for expenditure on activities;
- providing oversight and steering for the day-to-day management function;
- ensuring that management, monitoring and financial systems are in place;
- reviewing progress at regular intervals.

The chair of the partnership board does not necessarily have to come from the lead partner. Check whether board representatives need to have their decisions ratified by their own organisations before they can be considered 'binding'.

Management

This could be a single person or organisation or a team of people or organisations who are responsible for implementing and managing the partnership's activities from day to day. The management function should be independent. Its role is to implement the wishes of the board/decision-making group, not to pursue its own agenda. This is particularly important where the management function consists of people employed by one of the partners, or is perhaps located within the offices of a partner. Problems can sometimes arise if there is even a perception of bias and should be addressed as early as possible. A management team that is physically located in the premises of one of the partners will inevitably be associated with that partner's agenda, in perception if not actually. It is important to consider the implications of this.

Consultation or advice

This could be committees, subcommittees or a panel of project beneficiaries, whose role is to think, advise and offer feedback to the partnership. They may or may not be a formal part of the partnership. The role of any such committee or group or forum should be clearly set out and understood. It can have many different purposes and is often a useful way of exploring key issues in greater depth or involving stakeholders from outside of the partnership.

The role of the lead partner

There is a particular set of issues about the 'lead partner'. Many partnerships identify a lead partner and in many cases funding organisations (for instance, the European

Commission) require a lead partner to be nominated for contractual and financial accountability. For some partners the notion of having a lead partner can appear contradictory to their desire to be 'equal' partners. Equality of status, or of responsibility, or of voting rights, are all issues which your partnership will need to address – but they are not by themselves automatically impossible if a lead partner is nominated.

Lead partners often represent the public face of the partnership. Their role is to drive forward, not to dominate, the partnership's agenda. The partnership should clearly identify the role and remit of the lead partner as part of its discussions and deliberations at an early stage. Lead partners themselves will need to demonstrate that they can be trusted not to 'dominate' the partnership and exclude others from discussions.

Example: Communication and information exchange among partners

Consortium A's business plan noted that 'members of the consortium will keep in touch throughout the life of the project by e-mail and regular meetings, as appropriate.' A communications plan was agreed that included the annual progress reports and project development reports required by the funder, as well as individual project managers' highlight reports and ad hoc consortium communications. Systems were set up to facilitate ad hoc communications through a discussion list and to share consortium documents. These seem to have been effectively used only by the lead partner with few contributions by other partners.

Feedback and consultation between the lead partner and other partners, outside of consortium meetings, was through e-mail, telephone conversations and, most significantly, working

---

visits to partners by the consortium's educational consultant. At another level, however, informal communications – telephone and e-mail – between and among the partners was reportedly lively throughout the project, involving positive exchanges of information, expertise and perspectives on key areas of concern such as technology choices, technical development, web-writing and learning development.

A decision, based on practical considerations of time and efficiency, was taken by the lead partner to engage in minimal consultation on and sharing of information about the consortium budget and expenditure, beyond obtaining agreement from partners on specific activities to be paid for from the consortium budget. The reasoning behind this was that partners from different regions did not necessarily share the same perspective on what constituted value for money, and only the lead partner had significant experience in, for instance, contracting national level market research, marketing and web design services. With hindsight, this decision appears to have caused some disquiet among partners, and reinforced the impression that Consortium A and the project were being driven by the biggest, national partner, rather than being managed as a participatory initiative.

Maintaining the involvement of partners

The initial stages of partnership development tend to involve a lot of meetings and frenetic activity. As the relationships develop and as projects get bedded in, there is a period of settling down. SQW have identified the following risks in this stage:

- a greater focus on project delivery and less on strategic development;

- laziness or ambivalence about partnership processes and relationships;
- staff turnover and loss of experience and links;
- lack of attention to the partnership leading to lost opportunities;
- higher risk of implementation problems.

There are various ways to mitigate these risks.

Keep communicating

The key to keeping things going is to keep communicating – keep it regular but not routine, and keep it informative but without information overload. You may consider varying your usual approaches to meetings.

Preserving continuity

While this can be difficult, maintaining continuity of people is usually beneficial. Where individuals leave, try to ensure that some briefing and handover takes place with their replacements. Some partnerships even 'rotate roles' from time to time to ensure that individual people or organisations do not have just one particular kind of experience.

Checklist: Building partnerships

Establishing clear roles

- Are the roles and responsibilities of all partners clearly defined and agreed?
- Is there a lead partner?
- Is their role clearly defined and agreed?

Establishing an appropriate structure

- Has the partnership agreed an appropriate constitution and structure?
- Who employs staff?
- Who administers the day-to-day activities?
- Who contracts with delivery bodies?
- Which body makes the final decisions?
- Who is responsible for financial control and auditing?
- Is the membership of committees, working groups, etc. defined?
- Are there clear written procedures to prevent conflicts of interest?

Action planning

- Does the partnership have an action or business plan?
- Have those whose job it is to implement the project been involved in negotiating the action or business plan?
- Has the partnership carried out a risk assessment?

Notes and references

1. SQW Ltd. 'Working in partnership: a sourcebook'. See: *http://www.renewal.net/Documents/RNET/Research/Working partnershipsourcebook.pdf.*
2. From: *http://www.biglotteryfund.org.uk/er_eval_ict_final_rep .pdf.*
3. SQW Ltd, op. cit.

5

Assembling evidence in support of your proposal

Introduction

Most external funding organisations require a project rationale supported by some evidence that investment will be justified. This chapter considers what evidence might be needed and how it can be assembled, in particular evidence of appropriate needs or demand among target user groups or other project beneficiaries.

What do funding organisations require?

All project proposals will involve some kind of background research and supporting evidence to make their case for funding. If your project idea is to be funded from internal funds, as part of a programme of initiatives or innovations, then the evidence you need will, no doubt, be drawn mainly from internal sources – though you may still need to provide hard evidence of demand for 'customer-facing' services.

If you are proposing to enter into partnerships to seek external project funding you will certainly need to do some research and assemble some robust evidence in support of your funding application. Each potential funder will have their own particular requirements and a particular perspective. Here are four examples:

- The Heritage Lottery Fund is explicit in its Heritage Grants Application Form that it requires 'copies of research establishing a need or demand for your project'.

- The Joseph Rowntree Foundation is more discursive in its guidance for applicants – but it amounts to significant background research on the part of the applicant:

   You must place the proposed piece of work in the context of existing knowledge and/or practice, demonstrating a familiarity with the field and the relationship of your proposal to relevant recent or current work being carried out by others. You should also explain the extent to which the new project will relate to, or build upon, previous work. Demonstration projects must give details about the innovative nature of the work and the evidence that such a development is likely to be beneficial. Projects concerned to transfer good practice from one setting to another must also provide evidence that the practice is based on a sound assessment of 'what works'. Research proposals should indicate what gaps in knowledge the proposed project seeks to fill.

- At the high end of the funding scale, project proposals for 'large-scale integrating projects' in response to calls for proposals under the European Union (EU) Seventh Research Framework Programme in ICT Cooperation Applications are required to provide evidence of the project's likely 'progress beyond the state-of-the-art' entailing a description of the 'state-of-the-art in the area concerned, and the advance that the proposed project would bring about. If applicable, refer to the results of any patent search you might have carried out.'

- In another EU programme, eContentplus 2007, the Application Guidelines on completing the Technical Proposal forms require first 'analysis of demand' which 'should provide an analysis of the demand based as far as possible on quantified evidence'; and, second, a description of 'target users and their needs' which must 'for each category of target users, describe the unmet needs of the users'.

Some funding agencies that adopt a two-stage proposal and application process will provide modest upfront funds for applicants that get through the first, outline proposal stage, to enable them to do the research and business case development necessary for a full project proposal. Both the Heritage Lottery Fund and the Big Lottery Fund adopt this approach with some of their programmes. However, it is best to assume that, whether there is the prospect of additional funding or not, some significant and robust evidence gathering will need to be done in support of your project proposal. If you think it will be difficult to make staff and other resources or time available to undertake this research, you may need to consider other options, such as delaying your project development and submission or contracting in external assistance in the process. Make no mistake, competition for funding is so universally tough that the absence of robust supporting evidence will count heavily against your chances of success.

Information and evidence

Below is a range of different kinds of information and evidence that require research exercises to support your project proposal. It may also be that you would find some of these exercises essential in scoping and developing your project idea, as I suggest in Chapter 2. Some of them will be familiar to you and your organisation and the evidence you need may be readily available internally.

If you are entering into partnership with other organisations in your bid for project funding then you should be able to share the research and evidence-gathering burden between the partners – indeed, some of your existing or potential partners may be better placed to undertake some of these exercises in support of your project idea.

Environment scanning

The purpose of environment scanning is to identify issues that are likely to have an impact on your project or initiative and prepare for them. Its value in project development lies in helping you to formulate planning assumptions. Environment scanning should examine recent events and current conditions with the main purpose of spotting trends and general directions in your field of interest and assessing their future implications for your organisation and the project. This is certainly an exercise familiar to strategic planners, undertaken in many organisations on an ad hoc basis, typically triggered by events. Sheila Corrall provides the following 'Suggested steps for structuring scanning':[1]

1. Select and structure themes of interest and people to research them.
2. Collect and collate data, information and opinions from target sources.
3. Sort and sift information into relevant variables, with significant influence.

4. Analyse and assess variables, identifying critical factors with substantial impact.
5. Interpret and integrate information into planning assumptions.

In an analysis of the environment within which your potential project may be assessed and implemented the themes and key issues are likely to be fairly focused. They will almost certainly be easily addressed through desk research, covering key government, organisational and academic documentation – and, of course, websites – and a scan of recent, current and forthcoming research or project activity in the same or similar fields as your project. If it has a local or regional focus, environmental scanning is likely to be done primarily through consultation with colleagues and other local stakeholders – in meetings, informal communications, etc.

Despite the implications in time and effort, I would advise you to try to summarise your findings on each key theme or issue in a structured and formal way from the start, developing textual summaries, identifying and recording key references, etc. You will find it a great help to have this almost-final material to draw on, and it will save you a lot of time later on when you are finally writing your project proposal.

SWOT analyses

Though probably the most basic analysis method used in strategic planning, the SWOT (strengths, weaknesses, opportunities, threats) diagram can be a powerful and useful tool in identifying the main features of the situation when planning a new initiative. It can help you to identify not only your organisation's (or partnership's) key strengths or comparative advantages, but also point out the areas in which you may have information or evidence gaps.

In a SWOT analysis you draw a cross, creating four sectors and then enter in the relevant quadrant the strengths, weaknesses, opportunities and threats associated with the particular initiative you are planning. Figure 5.1 is an example taken from guidance on assessing a new business venture or proposition, but the criteria examples are useful nonetheless.[2]

Figure 5.1   Example of a SWOT analysis diagram

Criteria examples	Strengths	Weaknesses
Advantages of the proposal? Competitive advantages? Unique selling points? Resources, assets, people? Experience, knowledge, data? Likely financial returns? Outreach, awareness raising possibilities? Innovative aspects? Location? Price, value, quality? Processes, systems? Cultural, attitudinal, behavioural? Management issues? Philosophy, values?		
Criteria examples	**Opportunities**	**Threats**
Developments in the external environment? Lifestyle trends? Competitors' vulnerabilities? Technology developments? Global influences? Partnerships? Location or geographical changes? New products, services? New or changed resources? Economies?		

In doing your project SWOT analysis you should identify criteria that are appropriate to your project situation.

Developing a business case

A business case sets out the information needed to enable a manager to decide whether to support a proposed project before significant resources are committed to its development. The core of the business case is usually an assessment of the costs and benefits of proceeding with a project. In almost all cases, the option of doing nothing is also a part of the assessment, with the costs and risks of inactivity included along with the differences (costs, risks, outcomes, etc.) between doing nothing and the proposed project.

If you are developing a project proposal for internal funding, the preparation of a business case will almost certainly be required at an early stage. Some external funding agencies also require, if not a full business case, the kind of cost-benefit analysis or investment appraisal that it normally includes to show that the benefits of the project will outweigh the costs. While it is usually acceptable to use the approved method of analysis of your organisation or some other standard method, these kinds of analysis are not trivial tasks.

Cost-benefit analysis

This was developed as a means of establishing criteria for public sector investment in terms of net social benefit by, as far as possible, placing monetary values on social benefits. Cost-benefit studies typically try to determine the economic feasibility of alternative proposals for achieving defined objectives, by identifying both the monetary/financial and the opportunity/social costs and benefits. In effect, the aim is to justify a project or activity by demonstrating that the benefits outweigh the costs. The judgement of what qualifies as a 'benefit' becomes a critical issue; differing stakeholder perspectives of benefits will affect the way the analysis is viewed. Results can also be controversial because the determination of values for non-monetary and intangible costs and benefits is inevitably subjective. Nonetheless, as Sheila Corrall[3] says, it can 'be a useful means of forming a rounded view of all strategic and operational issues, even if quantification is not really practical.' While her approach to analysis is from a strategic planning point of view, her suggested steps (Table 5.1) and cost-benefit matrix (Figure 5.2) can also be applied to project planning and definition with some adaptation.

Table 5.1   Suggested steps towards cost-benefit analysis

1.	Identify the stakeholders who would benefit from and/or pay for the results of your project.
2.	Itemise the potential costs and benefits for each stakeholder group.
3.	Verify your assumptions with your colleagues and managers and selected members of stakeholder (user) groups.
4.	Consider how to measure or assess the value of each cost and benefit and use a matrix similar to the example in Figure 5.2, marking the relevant boxes with either a monetary value where it is possible to assign one, or a numerical score to indicate scale of benefit (e.g. 1 to 5, with 5 being of highest importance).
5.	Consult key stakeholders to clarify and verify the costs and benefit values you have assigned.
6.	Indicate net values and indicate whether the total benefits exceed total costs.

Figure 5.2	Cost-benefit analysis matrix example

	STAKEHOLDERS			
	Group A (e.g. service staff)	Group B (e.g. service users)	Group C	Group D
COSTS e.g.				
Accommodation/ storage				
Consumables				
Equipment				
Information resources				
Opportunity cost of time				
Staff salaries				
BENEFITS e.g.				
Increased use of resources/services				
Better informed decisions				
Community relations gains				
More timely information				
Productivity gains				
Higher organisational profile				
Psychological gains, e.g. raised staff morale, positive user responses				

Socio-economic assessment

It used to be very common, particularly in EU funding programmes, for grant applicants and project proposers to include a 'socio-economic assessment' of the impact and value of their proposed initiative or activities. This was almost always regarded by assessors as one of the weakest areas in funding applications, usually with good reason. Many organisations were at a loss to understand precisely what such an assessment required, and others realised that, to address the question seriously, considerable background and some original research was probably necessary, and this was hardly ever done.

Most external funders – including most EU funding programmes – have replaced the concept with requirements for some kind of appraisal of the economic and social implications of the proposed activity but you may still come across the term. In a project proposal or funding application context, it can best be interpreted as a considered appraisal of the social impact of the initiative in relation to the costs – this comes quite close to 'value-for-money' considerations and cost-benefit analyses.

Business plan

A business plan may share some of the features of a business case, but it is a more general and discursive document, which should clearly explain the what, why, when, who and how of the project. It should be a comprehensive explanation of the opportunity, the people involved, the money required to implement the plan, where that money will come from and what financial results the opportunity is likely to produce. In effect, developing the business plan is the summary of your project definition exercise. Many external funders will, at some stage, require a full business plan in addition to the fully completed application form despite considerable duplication between the two.

The New Opportunities Fund (before it became part of the Big Lottery Fund), for instance, suggested to second-stage applicants in the Digitisation of Learning Materials Programme that the following components should be included in a business plan, in addition to the detailed descriptions of the project aims, objectives, management and staff resources and work plan:

An analysis of the need, with figures of service users:

- Provide evidence which shows that there is a need and the demand for your project and that funding is not available from other sources.
- Try to make sure that statements about need and demand are backed by statistical evidence like data from local and national surveys, focus groups, market research, etc.

Survey of similar or related services and projects provided by other organisations:

- Detail the presence or absence of other local providers and its impact on your project; demonstrate, if possible that your project is filling a gap in the market.

Financial information:

- Income and expenditure projections for the duration of the project: the assumptions behind any projections should always be made explicit.
- Cash flow forecasts should also be prepared.

Market research

Most major funding agencies want some evidence of market research to support a project proposal. The library, archive and museum world has, until quite recently, been uncomfortable with the concept of the 'market' and sceptical that market research techniques, developed in the commercial sector, can be usefully applied in public sector services. It is still the case that we tend to prefer talking about 'user' or 'audience' research, and we are very prone to talking in general terms of the 'public' as if it were a homogenous mass.

> We talk about 'the public', or even the 'general public', without thinking very much about it. One dictionary definition of the public calls it 'the community as an aggregate', with 'community' meaning a body of people living in the same locality, and an 'aggregate' meaning a collection of units, in this case people, into one mass. 'The public' is also useful shorthand for purchasers or users in general. There is even a popular stereotype associated with it – called 'the man in the street' – who is usually understood to represent some sort of average person whom we think of in some way representative of the public – a sort of human mean.[4]

In reality, the generic term 'the public' is not much use if you are trying to identify the needs of particular groups for products or services. Needs, as Chapman and Cowdell say,[5] are first generated by individuals, each of which is a separate entity with his or her own tastes, preferences, desires and wants. For the same reason, the market, in commercial terms, is rarely a homogenous concept and it 'has long been recognised that the process of exchange is really like a long sorting process, through which individual products or services find their ways to individual purchasers or users.'

Market research techniques and methodologies offer libraries and the cultural heritage sector useful tools to define their communities and audiences more closely, and many cultural organisations now employ professional market researchers to assist them in applying the techniques. Probably the most useful concept to take from market research orthodoxy is 'market segmentation'. However, Chapman and Cowdell[6] identify one important distinction to be made between commercial consumer markets and public sector markets, the nuances of which often seem to get lost in market research outcomes:

> A consumer market consists of all those who buy or acquire goods and services for personal use. In practice, there is a distinction to be made between those who have the power to buy these goods and services directly and those who do not. This distinction is an important one for the public sector: on the one hand, there are services which provide for the wants of those who can afford to use them; on the other, there are services for which the demand is so obvious that limited resources must be managed ... This latter category will include provision for those who use public sector services because they cannot afford to do otherwise. However, they can still be defined and understood as market segments.

The concept of market segmentation can be easily described but putting it into practice is often more difficult. There are basically three steps:

1. Define the total market – for your project this may already mean a subdivision of your organisation's total market, e.g. the total population of a county, all the residents of and visitors to a particular city.

2. Divide that market into segments that are useful and appropriate to your organisation's strategic aims.

3. Select those segments of your market that are relevant to your project.

If we look more closely at the division of a market into segments, there are many ways of doing this: public service organisations tend to favour a 'user characteristics' approach which addresses the question 'who are the users (or potential users) of this service?' Typical ways to start are dividing your market by age, socio-economic groupings (often a surrogate for buying power) or geographical location. The 'user behaviour' approach, which asks the question 'what services do users need?' will also be familiar. Much market research in this area has been undertaken with the intention of finding out if there are enough similarities between the wants, needs and attitudes of individuals to identify viable groups or market segments. Elements of uniformity within groups are often reinforced by an existing *culture*, referring to a whole way of life or lifestyle of a group of people, rather than activities involving art, music and literature. Table 5.2 shows segmentation variables in this kind of division.

Table 5.2 Market segmentation variables in lifestyle

Activities	Interests	Opinions	Demographics
Work	Family	Personal	Age
Hobbies	Home	Social issues	Education
Social events	Job	Politics	Income
Holidays	Community	Business	Occupation
Entertainment	Recreation	Economics	Family size
Club membership	Fashion	Education	Dwelling
Community	Food	Products	Geography
activities	Media	Future	City size
Shopping	Achievements	Culture	Stage in life cycle
Sport			

Evidence of target beneficiary needs/demand

Within identified market segments – however you may define them – your project will have target users or beneficiaries. Clarity about exactly who your project will be aimed at, in the first instance, will be essential and this is where the techniques of market segmentation come in useful. It will be almost impossible to define achievable aims and objectives and assess the outcomes and impact of your project without this clarity and precision.

> Several of the Community Grids for Learning (CGfL) have large target groups – for instance, several local authority CGfLs interpreted 'community' as all adults living (or working) in the authority's area who might be interested in learning opportunities. While these may include groups with particular interests and needs, or who face particular problems in accessing learning opportunities, it is impossible to measure whether the CGfL has had any positive impact on them. Those CGfLs with coherent and focused targets have, on the whole, had more success in developing learning content and delivering information to meet community needs. [For instance:]
>
> When WEA-NW (Greater Manchester CGfL) replied to the Fund call for CGfL under the CALL programme in early 2000, it already had a clear vision of WEA's role in exploiting the potential of the new technologies in teaching and learning situations, clear aims and objectives for potential projects, identified target beneficiaries and partnership networks and experience in education and ICT.

This was due to the early involvement of WEA-NW in IT projects in the community in the 1990s and to its recognition of the importance of establishing medium-term objectives and strategies for potential online learning projects ... The CGfL Project aimed at developing interesting and relevant online content for key target groups. Most of the effort and time allocated to the project by the WEA-NW team was spent working with learners, tutors and community organisations to select course themes and content and to develop the online courses.[7]

Probably the most important type of evidence that you will need to assemble, which almost every external funder will require in some form or other, is evidence of your target user or beneficiary needs that justify your project idea. Unfortunately, and even after several years of experience in the project funding world, library, archive and museum organisations tend to fudge this exercise. Perhaps we feel we are continually surveying service users and asking for feedback about our services, or we are too often under pressure of time and resources and doing in-depth target user (and non-user) research seems too difficult, or perhaps we think we 'know our users' and their needs well enough already! User perceptions of benefit are very important, however, and we should recognise there may well be differences between users' views and ours, the service supplier.

[In the NOF Digitisation of Learning Materials Programme] many of the lead organisations (such as library services) had, within their main user groups, sub-groups and individuals that fitted the social inclusion targets, but these were not quantified. Target

user groups in the majority of projects were not
selected according to any particular lifelong learning
criteria. Despite the two-stage application process
intended, in part, to enable applicants to analyse more
fully the needs of their target audiences, it seems that
few projects undertook such analysis in systematic
ways.[8]

There is plenty of evidence around to suggest that, not only
will poor or non-existent target user research reduce your
chances of winning external funding, but also it will directly
constrain your chances of successfully defining your project
and implementing it for maximum benefit and positive
outcomes.

Where to start

To begin, you will need a good understanding of your target
audience's social and economic circumstances, the various
complexities of their lives, their aspirations, key
competencies and preferred learning styles, for instance.
Look for evidence elsewhere about these particular or
similar communities and their life circumstances, for
example in government or voluntary sector reports or in
research done in other sectors etc.

There is, however, no substitute for direct engagement
through participatory research with individual and
community beneficiaries. This will help you define the
project objectives, intended outcomes and desired impact,
and provide you with the evidence of demand and needs that
funders require. This kind of research means more than just
'consultation', and, though it may seem a difficult, time-
consuming and often frustrating exercise, in my view it

holds the key to successful projects with achievable and realistic goals.

> Whilst consultation is a valuable tool for library services, it was felt that engagement with communities should ideally go beyond consultation. Engagement involves local people in identifying areas for development and getting actively involved in delivering these improvements or additional services.[9]

The MLA, in its download library accompanying Inspiring Learning for All, provides useful 'guidelines on involving users'[10] and advises the following:

- Start with a blank sheet of paper and allow users to set the agenda.
- Don't rely on paper-based communication. Poor literacy and lack of English can provide a barrier to many users.
- Meet users at a time and place convenient to them, respecting their desire for confidentiality and informality. Libraries, museums and archives need to be willing to meet others on their terms and territory.

Research methods

Your choice of research techniques in target user needs research will depend on who they are and what resources you have. In most cases you are likely to use a mix of quantitative (e.g. surveys, gathering statistical data) and qualitative (e.g. focus groups, interviews, observation) methods. The mix will allow you to gather evidence in different ways to 'triangulate' or validate different research findings. Also bear in mind that this research, in the project definition or planning stages, should be robust enough not only to convince external funders of the need for your project, but also provide you with baseline data against which implementation progress and project outcomes can be assessed later.

In case you are tempted to rely on using only online research tools, e.g. online questionnaires, response and feedback mechanisms at your organisational website, etc., you should bear in mind that experience in the NOF Digitisation Programme indicated how difficult and often ineffective it is to engage with your target communities only online. Online surveys attract notoriously poor responses: web statistics can often be misleading as the underlying data and the data analysis techniques used may be flawed. I would suggest that nothing beats the personal touch of an interview or face-to-face conversation in establishing a target beneficiary's views and service needs.

Checklist: Evidence types

Environment scanning

- Desk and document-based research.
- Consult your colleagues and partners.
- Remember to summarise and record your findings well.

SWOT analysis

- Points out comparative advantages and information gaps.
- Use standard tools and develop your own analysis criteria.

Business case

■ Focuses on cost and benefit appraisal.

■ Check whether your organisation has methods and data you can use.

■ Involve your key project stakeholders and target beneficiaries.

Business plan

■ Should be written as a comprehensive preliminary to the final project plan.

■ Must include summaries of evidence gathered in support of your project.

Market research

■ Consider using market segmentation techniques as a preliminary to more in-depth user needs research.

■ User characteristics and user behaviour approaches are common in the public sector.

Target user or beneficiary needs research

■ Understand your target community's social and economic circumstances.

■ Consultation is not as robust as properly structured research using standard methods.

■ Online research methods are no substitute for face-to-face encounters.

Notes and references

1. Sheila Corrall (2000) *Strategic Management of Information Services: A Planning Handbook*. London: Aslib/IMI.
2. Adapted from SWOT analysis template – a free resource from Alan Chapman (2005) at: *http://www.businessballs.com*.
3. Corrall, op. cit.
4. David Chapman and Theo Cowdell (1998) *New Public Sector Marketing*. London: Financial Times & Pitman Publishing.
5. Ibid
6. Ibid.
7. From the evaluation of the NOF-Digitise and CGfL programmes at: *http://www.biglotteryfund.org.uk/er_eval_ict_final_rep.pdf*.
8. Ibid.
9. MLA and CSV Consulting (2006) *Community Engagement in Public Libraries: A Report on Current Practice and Future Developments*. April.
10. *http://www.inspiringlearningforall.gov.uk/utilities/download_library/index.aspx*

Setting project aims, objectives and outcomes

Introduction

Coherent aims, objectives and anticipated outcomes are the
backbone of every project – they provide clarity and focus,
and funders are likely to measure your progress and
achievements by them. While reviewing and, sometimes,
changing objectives during project implementation is
common practice, short-term projects (with a timescale of
under three years) do not allow for much flexibility of this
kind. Three years may seem like a long time at the start, but
the first six months can easily be taken up with
administrative matters and partnership dialogue while the
clock is ticking. The importance of setting the right
objectives from the start cannot be overstated.

Precision in formulating your aims, objectives and
expected outcomes, and careful and unambiguous choice of
words and phrases are also important – this is, after all, the
principle way (perhaps the only way) you will have of
communicating your project vision to potential funders and
stakeholders. Lack of ambiguity will also ensure that people
involved in implementing the project know exactly where
they are going and are able to review their progress against
something concrete and understandable.

This chapter provides some guidelines on setting and formulating realistic and achievable project objectives and outcomes.

Terms and meanings

It is probably a good idea to start by defining some terms, although this is not without its difficulties. Many of the terms relating to setting objectives can be used interchangeably and, while the terms you use are not significant in themselves, it is best to get everyone involved in project planning in your organisation using the same ones and meaning the same thing. Below are some suggested definitions.

Aims, goals, purpose

The goals, aim or aims of a project are usually a statement of its overall purpose, direction or where you want to get to at the end of the project. The project aim is likely to be quite broad, but take care that you are not aiming at something that will require more than your particular project to achieve it! For instance:

> The ERPANET project aims to establish an expandable European Network of Excellence, which will serve as a virtual clearinghouse and knowledge-base in the area of preservation of cultural heritage and scientific digital objects

is a good example of a big but nonetheless specific goal or purpose. On the other hand:

> Realisation and acknowledgement of the important function of the library as a crucial support to the

education, research and society development activities of the university as a fast growing, dynamic organisation facing major challenges

is over-ambitious and vague as the aim or 'overall objective' for a university library project focusing on library automation and the introduction of Internet-based information resources.

Objectives

Objectives are statements of achievements, attainable within the time-frame of the project, that will lead to the accomplishment of project goals. Objectives are operational statements; that is, they are written in terms that make it evident when they will have been achieved. As with aims and goals, they should be descriptions of a position rather than an action. As descriptions of a desirable future state, they will almost certainly imply a sequence of activities in order to achieve the desired future.

Below are two examples of project objectives: the first from the NOF Digitise PortCities Project Business Plan, and the second from the draft ERPANET[2] proposal for EU funding in 2001.

Example: PortCities objectives

1. Enhance the quality of life by providing new learning opportunities.
2. Widen access to maritime collections and knowledge through the medium of ICT.
3. Facilitate community capacity building, fostering a sense of identity at local, regional and national levels.
4. Encourage creativity and skills development among both users and project staff.

---

5. Improve employment and formal education prospects for individuals through the acquisition of both subject knowledge and ICT skills.

6. Promote active citizenship by including project materials that encapsulate responsible citizenship or can be used in educational contexts to prompt debate about the need to make informed choices in all aspects of civic life.

Example: Draft ERPANET objectives

1. To identify and raise awareness of sources of information about the preservation of digital objects across the broad spectrum of national and regional cultural and scientific heritage activity in Europe.

2. To appraise and evaluate information sources and documented developments in digital preservation on behalf of Network Members; and to make available results of research, projects and best practice.

3. To provide an enquiry and advisory service on digital preservation issues, practice, technology and developments.

4. To implement a suite of six development seminars to bring together experts from a range of disciplines to address key preservation issues (e.g. integrity and audit requirements, emulation and migration).

5. To build a suite of eight training workshops based on best practice (in such areas as building e-records procedures and policies, preservation of e-mail and web materials), and to identify where and what further practitioner training and staff development is required.

6. To develop a suite of tools, guidelines, templates for prototype instruments and best practice case studies.

7. To stimulate further research on digital preservation in key areas and encourage the development of standards where gaps and opportunities have been identified.

> 8. To build the membership of the Network step by step, inviting members to contribute to it, both in contents and resources, until it reaches a point at which it will be fully self-supporting.

Sheila Corrall[3] points out that objectives can be categorised into a hierarchy of five types: the first three types – purpose, function and direction objectives – are typical of organisational planning and strategic thinking. The objectives in the first example above from PortCities, despite being a set of project objectives, fit the 'direction objectives' category, being more general indications of desired movement, improvement and development. In the project business plan these objectives are accompanied by a set of 'key outcomes' which define the measurable aspects of the objectives. The second example above from ERPANET, on the other hand, fits the 'results objectives' category, which is one of the two types in Corrall's hierarchy that are more appropriate to project planning:

- *Results objectives* – answer the question 'what exactly do we want to achieve?' and will often incorporate forms of measurement or verification.

- *Task objectives* – answer the questions 'how will we do this?' and 'who will do this?' and tend to define specific activities.

Activities and tasks

These are specific targets representing the actions and actual deliverables required within the project timescale in order to fulfil the objectives and achieve the project aims. They are usually defined within project work plans, with their own set of 'task objectives' and activities, and tied to specific deliverables. The example in Figure 6.1 is from the draft ERPANET proposal (2001) work plan.

Figure 6.1 Example of a work package description

Work package: Project inception and management			
Work package number: 1			
Start date or starting event: Month 0			
Participant number: C1 C2 C3 C4			
Person-months per participant 16 1 1 1			

Objectives

This work package supports all the ERPANET Objectives:

(a) Identify and recruit for the Network a range of members in each of the four European Zones.

(b) Ensure that the management and decision-making structures of the ERPANET Network function effectively and are serviced efficiently.

(c) Ensure co-ordinated activity across all work packages through day-to-day correspondence [e-mail etc.], maintenance of document repositories, timetabling and agenda setting, etc.

(d) Assure the quality and consistency of all project deliverables.

(e) Ensure effective communication with the Commission and the timely provision of project progress reports and accurate cost statements.

Description of work

Task 1 – Make contact with relevant institutions and individuals to encourage active participation as Members.

Task 2 – Agreement among ERPANET Contractors on Membership nomination, procedures and terms.

Task 3 – Establish process for systematic acquisition of links to key documents, services and demonstrators, other relevant websites, including the negotiation of rights issues.

Task 4 – Ensure co-ordination of work across the whole network project, throughout its duration.

Figure 6.1   Example of a work package description (*cont'd*)

Task 5 – Organise and provide secretariat for team meetings and co-ordinate communications.

Task 6 – Collate Management, Progress Reports and Cost Statements for the European Commission.

Task 7 – Manage quality assurance, packaging and promotion of all ERPANET deliverables.

Task 8 – Co-ordinate communication and activities with related actions [e.g. DELOS].

Deliverables

D1 – Membership protocols and membership documents and a list of core members.

Inputs and outputs

Each one of these task objectives will have resource implications associated with it – a certain number of days by specific staff members or contractors will be required to undertake the task and achieve the objective; specific funds will need to be spent; equipment will need to be acquired and installed, etc. These are the project inputs – quantifiable and accountable, and usually estimated as part of the project work plan. Outputs are the quantifiable products or results of these inputs. They may be expressed as precise 'deliverables' or they may be aggregated results which meet the requirements of your task objective.

For instance, if one of your project's task objectives is to undertake a feasibility study, the inputs might be x number of days' effort by a member of staff or consultant plus funds to cover their expenses. The outputs then would be the required reports (which may or may not be specified project deliverables) plus any other manifestations of their work that were defined in their terms of reference for the task (e.g. workshops or presentations). Note that the *quality* of the reports or other manifestations is not at issue; only the existence or quantity of outputs is measured.

If, on the other hand, a task objective of your project were to improve student access to computers in a university department through the provision of appropriate advice and equipment, the inputs may be staff time in assessing the need and specifying the appropriate PCs and peripherals and, of course, the procurement of the actual hardware and software. In this case, the outputs would be x number of fully functioning PCs, supported by required peripherals, in use in the designated department.

Outcomes

Outcomes are quite different to outputs, although the words are often used interchangeably and erroneously. An outcome implies a qualitative aspect, and may be considered as a result of something else. Outcomes can rarely be measured using quantitative data; if it can be counted it is generally an output not an outcome.

To extend my previous example, an outcome of the feasibility study report and other presentations mentioned above, which were the *outputs* of the project's task objective, might be a unanimous decision on the part of the project board to go ahead with the project or the setting up of a working group to redefine the project plan, all of which would be based on recommendations in the study's outputs – the report and presentations.

Similarly, the provision of x number of PCs and peripherals in the university department, the output in my second example above, might lead to several outcomes, including an increase in student numbers working in the department, and more positive feedback from students and staff.

You should normally have specific outcomes in mind when you set your objectives and plan your activities, although it is worth bearing in mind that every task objective and activity in a project will have both anticipated and unanticipated outcomes.

Impact

Outcomes and impact are very hard to untangle and the terms are frequently used as if they were interchangeable, but they are not. Peter Brophy and Susi Woodhouse provided a useful definition for NOF Digitisation:[5]

> Outcome measures relate to those things which happen as a result of the outputs. So the web pages [the output] accessed will, hopefully, lead to some at least being read [the outcome].
>
> It is when we start to measure impacts that the real answers begin to emerge. The question[s] that must be answered [include] 'What good does this resource do?' or 'What difference has it made?' ... These are the most valuable measures of all – but they are also the most difficult.

For example, a learning outcome might be what you wanted your target audience to do or achieve as a result of your project; the impact of that learning outcome would be what happened to them as a result, or how the outcome changed them.

The impact of projects and their activities is often hard to predict or to anticipate. You may have started out with a broad view of what kind of impact you want to make on your target beneficiaries, but you may only be able to control the outputs and outcomes of your project – impact is usually subject to a much wider range of social, economic and cultural factors, and often manifests over a period of time too long to be encompassed within the project itself.

Setting objectives

First and foremost, your project objectives need to be shaped by your project's target beneficiaries, making the needs research evidence and consultation exercises you will have undertaken in the preparatory stages (see Chapter 5) of vital importance.

Secondly, objectives must take account of the broad resources available in the planned project. There is little point in setting objectives that are beyond the limited scope of your potential funding or impossible to achieve within a limited project time frame. Consider, for example, the unrealistic nature of the objectives below that were included in the terms of reference for a consulting project of a mere 21 person-days' input over one year, as part of the World Bank-funded Education Improvement Project in Lithuania.

The Consultant must:

- assist the Working Group (WG) in preparing standard specifications of teaching aids to ensure suitability of the teaching aids to the national curriculum and local conditions;
- assist the WG in formulating criteria for assessment of effectiveness of the teaching aids used for the teaching and learning process and in preparing an assessment questionnaire;
- provide the WG with up-to-date knowledge and information of pedagogical usage (educational methods) of teaching aids in learning;

- acquaint the WG with products of reputable international manufacturers producing quality teaching aids including teaching aids intended for students with physical and learning disabilities (provide catalogues/price lists of products);
- evaluate the material prepared by sub-component one 'Teaching aids' and ensure that they are in line with other sub-components;
- assist the WG in preparation of the catalogues/price lists of teaching aids, based on the school's needs;
- propose a potential model of the national system of provision with teaching aids.

Thirdly, it is important to remember that setting project objectives is an iterative process – your final, documented objectives are likely to look very different to your first attempt, after you have reviewed them at each step in the project preparation process and shared them with a range of project stakeholders. They will perhaps have been revised by your top management or your partners to fall more closely in line with organisational goals, been pared down after the implications of budget constraints on activities have become clear, been reordered to meet the requirements of partner priorities and been reassessed in the light of a more realistic understanding of time constraints.

Check the efficacy of your objectives

A commonly used mnemonic, useful for checking the efficacy of objectives statements, is SMART. On this basis, objectives should be:

- *Specific* – in terms of desired results and responsibility for delivery.

- *Measurable* – either quantitatively or by demonstrating qualitative achievement.
- *Acceptable* – to stakeholders (ideally agreed with and owned by them).
- *Realistic* – in relation to environmental factors and available resources.
- *Time-bound* – according to the particular project context.

Your project objectives should also be *consistent* with your own organisation's mission and philosophy, *compatible* with each other so that there is no duplication or contradictions between your stated objectives, and *unambiguous* in their wording, avoiding the use of jargon or acronyms that may not be clear to the wider community or potential funders.

Below are three examples to test these checks on objectives. The first is from the gallery and archive Belfast Exposed, which successfully bid for NESTA funding to fund their Gateways project. Gateways will produce an easy-to-use collection browser with an interactive function, history of photography section and workshop presentation package builder – combining all areas of Belfast Exposed activity – the exhibition programme, the archive and workshop activity. The project planned the key aims and objectives shown in Table 6.1. I have commented on each of them in terms of the SMART and other suggested checks.

The second example is a set of objectives and key outcomes for a training programme of ten weeks duration for international librarians run by an academic institution in Europe, with participants from all over the world. The objectives listed in Table 6.2 together with my comments reflect the anticipated variety of participants' knowledge base, experience and levels of expertise.

Table 6.1 Example of aims and objectives from Belfast Exposed

Key aims	Comments
1. Develop an intuitive browser facility	Specific and measurable. Is it clear to everyone what intuitive means in this context?
2. Pioneer new content management systems (CMS) to challenge the closed character of the archive and gallery	Not specific about number of CMS that will be tested and/or used. Use of word 'challenge' is ambiguous – what exactly will the appropriate CMS achieve?
3. Continue creative partnerships around innovative approaches to access	Not specific enough to be measured.
4. Develop new ideas for the sector	How can this aim be assessed or measured? What is a 'new idea' in this context?
5. Work in partnership with historical photography archives to develop a History of Northern Irish Photography section of the browsing facility	Is this consistent and compatible with Key aim 3 above? How is this partnership different?
6. Broaden access to gallery and collection and enhance outreach capacity	Not specific enough about, for example, target audience groups.
Objectives	**Comments**
Encourage greater dialogue around the photographs	Can this be measured quantitatively or qualitatively?
Create a tool for lifelong learning	Not specific enough either about what sort of 'tool' or 'lifelong learning'.
Contextualise and open up Belfast Exposed's archive	Is this consistent with Key aims 2 and 6 above? Are they repetitive?
Permit greater understanding of the way archives work	Ambiguity around the meaning of 'archive' in this context – does it mean a generic archive? Is this consistent with the outcome immediately above? How can this be measured?

Table 6.1   Example of aims and objectives from Belfast Exposed (*cont'd*)

Objectives	Comments
Promote greater understanding of the history of photography in Northern Ireland	Not specific enough about target audience groups. How can this be measured?
Support greater and more critical response to Belfast Exposed's exhibitions	Can this be measured? Is it a realistic objective for the Gateways project?
Raise profile and attract broader interest in Belfast Exposed	Does this duplicate the objective immediately above? Is this a realistic and measurable objective?
Inform and enhance existing Belfast Exposed outreach programme	Repeats Key aim 6 above? How can this be measured?

Table 6.2   Example of objectives from an international training programme for librarians

Objectives	Comments
1. To provide participants with a clearer view on the importance of information in general and for their environment in particular, and on how to manage information	Realistic certainly, but too open-ended and general? How will it be measured – through self-assessment by participants?
2. To teach the participants to cope with modern technology, in view of the increasing importance of ICT	Not sufficiently specific given that the emphasis throughout is on Internet access. Implies the possibility of wide range of ICT skills upgrading.
3. To guide them in retrieving information that is publicly accessible on an international scale	Very open-ended, presumably intended to enable different participants to focus on different kinds of information.
4. To teach them to store, organise, present, manage and publish information resources at personal, institutional, regional and national level	Is this objective realistic within the time frame of the training programme? The implication is that all of these aspects will be covered only superficially.

| Table 6.2 | Example of objectives from an international training programme for librarians (cont'd) |

Key outcomes	Comments
Every participant will have improved their ability to:	
1. Appreciate and explain the importance of access to information for their organisation	Ambiguous choice of words.
2. Present information to users and potential users, using appropriate technology	Ambiguous use of 'present' – does it really mean deliver or disseminate, or does it imply some kind of mediation and repackaging?
3. Train interested persons in the use and management of information, using appropriate presentation techniques	Is this a realistic outcome? There is no reference in the objectives to addressing training skills and techniques.
4. Contribute to the planning of the development of an information service	Is this outcome consistent with the objectives?
5. Communicate through the Internet with users of information, information providers, colleagues, etc.	Presumably a key outcome of Objective 2 above.
6. Apply quantitative methods in decision-making related to information systems and services	Ambiguity and lack of clarity – does not directly relate to any objective.

Finally the third example is taken from an EU Tempus Programme proposal to support the development of improved graduate studies and research management within a university in Albania (see Table 6.3). The project was to be implemented in three years.

| Table 6.3 | Example from a Tempus proposal for a UK–Albania partnership |

Objective	Comments
1. Stimulate awareness and debate on graduate studies and research management issues among university staff and students	How will this be measured?
2. Improve quality in the management of graduate studies and research programmes in social sciences	Not sufficiently specific – the terms 'quality' and 'management' are too general.
3. Create, within social sciences, a model infrastructure for the organisation, management and administration of academic research	Specific, but is it realistic within the timescale of the project?
4. Establish in Graduate School of European Studies a University Centre of Excellence in graduate studies and research management	What criteria will be used to define 'Centre of Excellence'? Is this realistic within the timescale?
5. Write and develop a series of best practice tools and guidelines for the management of graduate studies and research	Specific and probably achievable.
Key outcomes	Comments
1. Identification of priority issues among staff and student stakeholders	An outcome of Objective 1 that is measurable.
2. Communication and understanding between staff and students on key issues in graduate studies and research planning and management	Does this duplicate Key outcome 1 above?
3. Transfer of expertise, experience, new skills and capabilities among up to 80 academic and administrative staff to plan, manage and deliver graduate programmes	How will this be measured?

| Table 6.3 | Example from a Tempus proposal for a UK–Albania partnership (cont'd) |

Key outcomes	Comments
4. Sustainable and appropriate library and research facilities for >300 graduate students, researchers and staff in the Faculty of Social Sciences and Graduate School of European Studies	Specific and measurable once 'sustainable' and 'appropriate' are defined.
5. Governance and management structures for graduate studies and research in the Graduate School of European Studies and Faculty of Social Sciences which are replicable in other subject disciplines	This duplicates and clarifies to some extent Objective 3 above – is there a need to separate these into an objective and an outcome?
6. Increased knowledge and understanding of European research programme management and quality assurance options and models among target groups	Not consistent with the objectives above – there is no specific mention of addressing European options and models. Ambiguity in the use of 'target groups' – which are these?

Notes and references

1. *http://www.portcities.org.uk/*
2. *http://www.erpanet.org/*
3. Sheila Corrall (2000) *Strategic Management of Information Services: A Planning Handbook*. London: Aslib/IMI.
4. *http://www.portcities.org.uk/*
5. Peter Brophy and Susi Woodhouse. *Evaluation and Impact Assessment for NOF Digitise Projects* at: *http://www.ukoln.ac.uk/nof/support/help/papers/impact-assessment/*.

7

Project planning

Introduction

Planning is an extension of the type of activity undertaken in project definition (see Chapter 2). If the project is long and complex then planning will take some time. Project planning is not an easy process and it may be tempting to make a sketchy plan, get started on the project and respond to events as they come up. I would strongly advise against this! Careful planning and review of plans before embarking on any activity is really worth the effort.

> When the Unnetie project was planned, the Library and Information Service was part of the Education and Libraries Directorate of the North Yorkshire County Council (NYCC). The project website was developed as an integral part of the NYCC corporate web presence, and the project team had minimal control over functionality and design.
>
> With hindsight, the project team realised that they should have taken more time to develop a content and technical plan before starting to digitise images. Likewise, with hindsight they would have benefited from the involvement of the NYCC IT staff much earlier in the project planning and application stage, and thus they might have avoided some of the subsequent

difficulties in communication and collaboration on the technical aspects of the project. While the project officer had significant experience in web-based content projects, she only joined the team in early 2002, after the official start date, and was never able fully to control the technical development.[1]

It is useful as a start to revisit the essential characteristics of a project that are represented in a project plan. These can be summarised as a triangle in which the angles represent cost, time and performance, circumscribed by regulatory or external constraints, as shown in Figure 7.1.

The point to bear in mind is that, as with any triangle, you cannot change one angle without affecting one or both the others. For instance, the timescale of your project cannot be changed without affecting either cost or performance or both. Projects are also planned and implemented against a background of risk as well as external constraints, about which you can make considered assumptions but which you cannot control.

Figure 7.1   Essential characteristics of projects

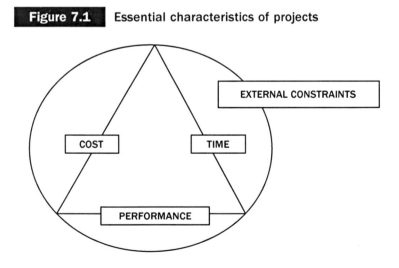

This chapter considers what needs to be included in a project plan, some useful planning techniques, and how risks can be assessed and incorporated into the planning process.

Project planning activities

The origin of the project plan is the outline definition, the agreed aims, objectives and broad outcomes. Project planning can be broken down into the following activities:

- Review the project aims, objectives and required outcomes.
- Analyse the work content into work packages and tasks.
- Consider effort and duration of each task and elapsed time.
- Determine the logical sequence for each work package, its prerequisites and outcomes (scheduling).
- Construct a project timetable based on the schedule.
- Consider and then cost the resources required to complete each activity and work package.

Reviewing the project objectives

It's always a good idea to revisit your project objectives after an interval to try to assess them in a fresh light, or get someone else who has not been directly involved in the definition of the project to assess them with a degree of objectivity, to see whether they are indeed SMART (see Chapter 6) and whether they make sense within policy and other contexts. The key issue to consider, when reviewing your objectives, is whether it is clear what the critical success factor or factors will be for each one – in other words, what *outcomes* must be manifest at the end of the project for the project to be considered a success.

In each project – and possibly for each objective of the project – there is likely to be a range of success factors or outcomes, some of which will be essential and some merely desirable. Deciding on the outcomes and their level of priority provides a measure for project evaluation (see Chapter 9) and also helps to identify the critical tasks in project planning.

Work content and task analysis

Work packages

Establishing the work content for a project requires the identification of the high-level critical tasks or activities required to achieve each objective. As an example, let's look again at three of the objectives drafted for the ERPANET proposal in 2001.

1. To identify and raise awareness of sources of information about the preservation of digital objects across the broad spectrum of national and regional cultural and scientific heritage activity in Europe.
2. To appraise and evaluate information sources and documented developments in digital preservation on behalf of Network Members, and to make available results of research, projects and best practice.
3. To provide an enquiry and advisory service on digital preservation issues, practice, technology and developments.

The success factors or essential outcomes of these objectives could be:

- high-quality information sources identified relevant to digital preservation across Europe;

- effective collection of peer-reviewed high-quality content;
- provision of effective access to information and content for target beneficiaries;
- improved levels of awareness of European best practice and key issues among target beneficiaries.

To achieve those outcomes the high-level critical tasks, therefore, are likely to include

- identification and assembling of high-quality content and information;
- presentation and provision of access to content and information in user-friendly formats;
- promotion and dissemination of assembled content and information to target beneficiaries.

These high-level activities can then be further developed into three 'work packages', each with its own sub-objectives as follows:

Work package: Adding content

This work package will work towards the achievement of ERPANET's Objectives 1, 2 and 7.

Objectives

(a) Identify information sources, collect and evaluate a range of relevant documents, standards, technical guidelines, research reports and web-published material, produced nationally or internationally in each of the four identified Zones.

(b) Review and appraise relevant research and development projects and related actions under EU Framework

---

Programmes, US NSF and other national and international funding programmes, and in the commercial and industrial sectors; establish links and referrals as appropriate.

(c) Monitor new ICT industry and research developments on behalf of Members.

(d) Expand web-based access to growing information repository and disseminate information on new materials through Network bulletins and updating services.

Work package: Technology infrastructure and instruments

This work package supports the whole project and provides specific input to ERPANET's Objectives 2 and 6.

Objectives

(a) Generate the underlying technical infrastructure for ERPANET.

(b) Establish an extensive web-based service, including local web pages for each Zone.

(c) Maintain and expand the ERPANET website and access to the information repository and ERPANET products and services.

(d) Identify and agree evaluation procedures and quality assessment criteria for appraisal of information sources and documents.

(e) Design and pilot templates for data collection in the research and development of case studies in best practice across the sectors served by ERPANET.

Work package: Service and product development and delivery

This work package supports the achievement of ERPANET's Objectives 2, 3 and 6.

Objectives

(a) Research and develop five best-practice case studies per Zone per year, making these available in English translations on the Network; translate and produce English and other language summaries/abstracts of key documents, as appropriate.

(b) Develop reference models, metadata sets and/or sets of requirements.

(c) Develop a suite of tools, guidelines and instruments for members, focusing initially on three aspects of digital preservation: costing preservation strategies, selecting technology and policy building.

(d) Develop other services responsive to members' needs, including:

- an enquiry and advisory service;
- web-based delivery of information, documentation, tools and guidelines;
- bulletin board (using web-board technologies) and discussion lists.

Thus we see that a 'package' of work is a fairly big chunk of a particular kind of activity. The work package 'Adding content', for instance, is activity related to the identification, acquisition and review of information and content from a wide variety of sources and in a variety of formats. Note also that each work package can often contribute to several of the project's objectives: work packages are concerned with the operational aspects of the project rather than the aspirational.

They describe what needs to be done to put aims and objectives into practice and achieve favourable outcomes.

Task analysis

As shown in the examples above, each work package should have its own sub-objectives, which themselves break down the overall or broad activity. These in turn should then be further broken down into a set of key tasks or chunks of work.

Following on with our previous example, therefore, here are the main tasks associated with each of the three ERPANET work packages:

Work package: Adding content

Description of work

Task 1 – Management meetings to clarify scope, establish methodologies, etc.

Task 2 – Identification and review of literature, published standards, research and policy documentation from four European Zones, North America, Australia and Asia.

Task 3 – Interviews and consultation in four European Zones among library, archive and museum and ICT industry constituencies by Content Editors.

Task 4 – Identification, collection and translation (where necessary) of key documents.

Task 5 – Web search and follow-up on R&D projects and related actions.

Work package: Technology infrastructure and instruments

Description of work

Task 1 – Implement the technological infrastructure.

> *Task 2* – Design website and templates for local web page creation.
> *Task 3* – Set up, maintain and publicise ERPANET website and Zone-specific pages.
> *Task 4* – Provide basic training in web page creation etc. to Consortium Contractors.
> *Task 5* – Design and pilot templates for data collection, case studies and other instruments.

Work package: Service and product development and delivery

Description of work

Task 1 – Management meetings to guide the development of a range of key services and products.
Task 2 – Plan services and products.
Task 3 – Implement services and products.
Task 4 – Make products and services accessible.

Each work package should have some identified outputs or 'deliverables' – not to be confused with outcomes! These will be specific and quantifiable things such as:

Work package: Adding content

Deliverables

- Mediated content and information sources posted on ERPANET website.

Work package: Technology infrastructure and instruments

Deliverables

- Technical infrastructure including functioning website, web-boards and underlying database management services and systems.
- Set of procedures and criteria for content building.

Work package: Service and product development and delivery

Deliverables

- Bulletin board and discussion lists available to members.
- Sets of case studies posted on the website.
- Enquiry and advisory service available for members.
- First tools, guidelines and practitioner aids made available to Network members.

A final word on work packages – do not forget to address the overall task of project management as a work package, along with other project activities. You will need to be very clear on what the objectives of the work of project management should be and what the key tasks involved will be. The example below shows what might be included.

Work package: Inception and project management

Objectives

This work package supports all the ERPANET Objectives.

(a) Identify and recruit for the Network a range of members in each of the four European Zones (see Part C5).

(b) Ensure that the management and decision-making structures of the ERPANET Network function effectively and are serviced efficiently.

(c) Ensure coordinated activity across all work packages through day-to-day correspondence [e-mail etc.], maintenance of document repositories, timetabling and agenda setting, etc.

(d) Assure the quality and consistency of all project deliverables.

(e) Ensure effective communication with the Commission and the timely provision of project progress reports and accurate cost statements.

Description of work

Task 1 – Make contact with relevant institutions and individuals to encourage active participation as Members.

Task 2 – Agreement among ERPANET Contractors on Membership nomination, procedures and terms.

Task 3 – Establish process for systematic acquisition of links to key documents, services and demonstrators, other relevant websites, including the negotiation of rights issues.

Task 4 – Ensure coordination of work across the whole Network project, throughout its duration.

Task 5 – Organise and provide secretariat for team meetings and coordinate communications.

Task 6 – Collate management, progress reports and cost statements for the European Commission.

Task 7 – Manage quality assurance, packaging and promotion of all ERPANET deliverables.

Task 8 – Coordinate communication and activities with related actions [e.g. DELOS, DLM-Forum].

Duration and effort

Having broken down the work into packages and identified the main tasks you need to think about how long each of them might take (in days, weeks, months) and how much effort they might require (in person-days, person-weeks or person-months). These two concepts of duration and effort can be confusing because the basis for calculating them both is usually the same – how long the work will take to complete. It might take, for instance, one member of staff working alone on a task six days to complete the work: that would be six days in duration and six days of effort. However, if two members of staff are deployed to work together on the same task it should only take three days to complete it – the duration of that task will then have been three days, but still six days in terms of effort.

Duration

Some tasks are unit-based, for instance there is a known number of books to be catalogued; the time taken for each unit can be measured and multiplied to give the likely duration of the task.

> Be realistic – say that a working day is eight hours and it takes 15 minutes on average to catalogue a book. It does not follow that one person can catalogue 32 books in a day! That would allow no time to take their coats off, talk to colleagues about the awful journey they have had, make a cup of coffee (and other essentials) or to think about what they are doing, answer queries from the enquiry desk or discuss a classification number with their boss. In calculating how long tasks take most planners assume between 60% and 70% efficiency – so it is more reasonable to expect our cataloguer to get through around 20 books in an average day.[2]

Other tasks are activity-based, that is the task is a single unit and it takes as long as it takes. Experience will tell you how long it takes to develop and pilot a questionnaire or to write a report. Sometimes it is very difficult to estimate duration accurately. Liz MacLachan suggests that one way of coping with this is to use the PERT method of estimating – to do this work out for each task:

- O – the most optimistic estimate of time;
- L – the most likely estimate of time;
- P – the most pessimistic estimate.

The duration will be (O + [4 × L] + P)/6. So if you think it will probably take 15 days to analyse the replies to a questionnaire and if you work hard it might take only 8, but on the other hand if something else crops up it might take 20 – then the likely duration is (8 + [4 × 15] + 20)/6 or 14.6 days.

This task duration may be split up across a period of elapsed time so that the length of time it actually takes to complete the task may be considerably longer than its particular duration – see scheduling below.

Effort

If the task in hand is a fairly routine and repetitive one then the number of members of staff that can be devoted to it will directly affect its duration. However, this may not always be true with more complex, activity-based tasks: they may be tasks that only one person has the skills to do and dividing the work up between a number of different people may have an adverse effect on quality.

You may also have several staff at different levels of seniority (and therefore attracting different costs) contributing small amounts of time to a task during its implementation. Let's take the development and implementation of a questionnaire survey as an example: here is a set of tasks that might be required to achieve this:

1. Decide on the purpose of the questionnaire and what you want to ask.
2. Decide on the distribution and analysis methods.
3. Develop a set of questions and pilot or test them.
4. Refine the questions and design the format of the questionnaire.
5. Identify the sample of respondents to receive the questionnaire.
6. Send out the questionnaire and monitor returns.
7. Analyse the resulting data.
8. Write the report.

You will need to make a judgement about how much time (in person-days) will be required from staff members at different levels and the total effort required to complete the project will be the sum total of all their contributions. Table 7.1 illustrates the example.

Scheduling

Staging

It is likely that your project will fall fairly naturally into different stages, with perhaps one or two work packages assigned to each stage – e.g. feasibility, development, testing and appraisal, or preparation, desk research, research implementation, analysis and synthesis. Staging is usually essential to organise and control more complex projects. A very large project will be planned in many stages, each of them like mini-projects on their own – each having to be

Table 7.1	Effort (in person-days) required at different staff levels to complete a questionnaire survey

Task	Senior manager	Middle managers	Administrative assistant	Total effort
1. Decide on the purpose of the questionnaire and what you want to ask	1	2		3
2. Decide on the distribution and analysis methods	0.5	1	0.5	2
3. Develop a set of questions and pilot or test them	0.5	2	2	4.5
4. Refine the questions and design the format of the questionnaire		2	1	3
5. Identify the sample of respondents to receive the questionnaire		2	3	5
6. Send out the questionnaire and monitor returns			5	5
7. Analyse the resulting data		2	4	6
8. Write the report	0.5	4		4.5
Total person days	2.5	15	15.5	33

scheduled so that all the necessary steps are completed in time for the next stage.

Milestones

Within each project you should build in critical points where there may be a review of progress against the project plan.

These are milestones – significant events or decision points in your project. They are frequently used as payment points by the funding organisation once a satisfactory progress report or review has been completed. If your project is organised in stages then it is usual to have a milestone at the end of each stage. Simple milestone charts, presented in columns showing short verbal descriptions with planned and actual completion dates provide a useful summary.

Work package sequences

In your project work plan you will need to order the work packages so that dependencies and overlaps between activities are clear and logical. The structure of the draft ERPANET work plan provides an example:

The work programme will be carried out in seven work packages each designed to address one aspect of the overall project:

Work package 1 (Project inception and management) covers the start-up activities for the Network and ongoing network management implementing over 36 months.

Work package 2 (Technology infrastructure and instruments) establishes the technology infrastructure (web-based) for ERPANET and initiates a number of procedures and instruments for Consortium Contractor activities in subsequent work packages.

Work packages 3 (Adding content) and **4** (Service and product development and delivery) are the central activities of the Network Contractors, focusing on building quality assured content as a knowledge resource and activity database, conducting case studies in sectors to enable sharing of best practice and cross-fertilisation, and developing a range of services and products for Network members and non-members. They represent continuous activities implementing for almost the duration of the project.

Work package 5 (Development seminars) covers one of ERPANET's major outcomes: a series of development seminars for members and non-members on leading-edge topics in digital preservation.

Work package 6 (Best-practice training workshops) represents the second major output of the Network: a series of training workshops for practitioners.

Work package 7 (Sustainability measures) ensures the long-term sustainability of ERPANET's work, and the quality and widespread impact of the Network's services and products.

Elapsed time

Duration is a useful measure of how long an individual task might take but it does not tell us how long the overall project will be – some of the tasks run in parallel and some overlap. Total time from the beginning to end (of a task, work package, stage or whole project) is elapsed time.

Delay is usually deliberately built into a project and is called slack. It is always sensible to build in slack since it provides useful reflection time and tasks will inevitably run over time! A different sort of delay is called lead time which occurs between dependent tasks. If, for example, you are decorating a room you will need to let the paint dry before you hang the paper. Overlapping tasks have an inbuilt lag – you need to allow time for the questionnaire to be returned before you can start to analyse the results.

Timetabling

Once all the work packages, tasks, their duration and their relationship to each other have been identified the project timetable is created by giving each their start and finish dates. This exercise is greatly assisted by the use of project management tools that create Gantt charts (see Chapter 8). Most projects have to be completed by a certain date, so it is helpful when you create your timetable to start at the end with the completion date for the project and work backwards, slotting in each task with its dependencies and each of the milestones in turn.

Estimating costs and setting budgets

To create your project cost estimates you will need to have completed the project work plan, calculated the resources required (e.g. labour, equipment, expenses) and allocated them to each work package and task. For the budget you will work out how much these resources will cost and in which period (usually months) you expect the costs to fall. The principles of financial forecasting and budgeting for projects are not significantly different to those in operational budgeting. As with core business operations, managing project costs and project spend is one of the ways the project will be monitored so getting the cost estimates and budget right from the start is important.

Project costs usually fall into three broad categories:

- people, your own staff and others (such as subcontractors) required for a particular task;
- equipment (including computer hardware and software);
- expenses or consumables (sometimes called reimbursables).

Many funding organisations provide specific instructions on how the costs should be worked out and presented: for example, here are some instructions from JISC.

> A summary of the proposed budget which in broad outline identifies how funds will be spent over the life of the project. The budget should be broken down across academic years (August–July) or parts thereof and should include itemised staff costs, any equipment and consumables, travel and subsistence, dissemination, evaluation, and any other costs required. All costs must be justified. TRAC methodology must be used to calculate costs in bids from UK HEIs with institutional contributions determined by taking into account the benefits to the lead institutions and any project partners. Bidders should provide a summary of the qualitative and any quantitative benefits the lead institution and any project partners expect to receive from the project, in order to inform the funding requested from JISC and the costs being borne by the host institution and any project partner. An example budget and guidance on the budgetary terms used can be found at Annex C. Non HEIs should use their institution's normal costing methods to determine any indirect costs.[3]

People

People costs are the largest element in library projects. Some organisations do not cost their own staff against a project arguing that their salary would need to be paid anyway. In my view this is a mistaken approach, which can contribute to projects being thought of as 'marginal' to the work of the organisation. Full staff costs associated with a project should always be calculated and included. To calculate staff costs, take the annual cost of each person and divide by the number of working days to get the daily rate. These calculations can be complicated, however, especially if your organisation has set no precedents on how to proceed or the funding organisation has provided no specific guidelines. For instance, how many days does your organisation calculate as a working year? The figure is usually between 210 and 220. Do you use salary cost or the full cost of employing that person? Full costs include on-costs and possibly an organisational overhead, so this can work out at almost double the salary cost.

What about indirect costs or overheads? Your organisation may have a policy of allocating a fixed overhead to labour costs (e.g. 20 per cent of direct costs) or it may have a standard formula to determine what the overhead should be. Some funding organisations themselves impose a fixed overhead rate on project labour costs (several EU funding programmes adopt this practice).

If your project is long and multi-dimensional the unit cost for people you may be using could be a person-week rather than a person-day, or even a person-month. In aggregating the calculated daily rate for your different members of staff you will need to be clear on what basis you have calculated your weeks and months – a working week of five days, or a full week of seven days? An average working month of 18–20 days or an average full month of 28–30 days?

Equipment

Equipment costs should be straightforward. However, if your project is going to run for more than, say, two years, you may need to consider amortisation of the costs of any durable equipment. Amortisation means you take into account in the project budget the fact that equipment depreciates over a period of time (the amortisation period) and if you need the equipment for a shorter period than this then you need to pay for the benefit of having it once the project is over. Your own organisation and many funding organisations will have a policy on the amortisation of different kinds and values of equipment: if you buy some equipment, for instance, for a two-year project and the amortisation period is three years, then you have to absorb the penalty for the third year. There are different ways to work out the depreciation rate of equipment, but the following method seems to be widely applied, according to Kirsten Black:[4]

Claimable amount = Cost of equipment × (Time to project completion)/(Amortisation period)

Here is an example using this formula:

Cost of equipment	£3,000
Amortisation period	36 months
Duration of project	24 months
Purchase date of equipment	Month 3

Claimable amount = £3,000 × ((24 − 3)/36) = £1,750

Obviously, when you are planning the project you should schedule the purchase of equipment as close to the start of the project as possible to take best advantage of the depreciation rate.

Don't forget to include an element for maintenance costs if your project lasts more than a few weeks. Ten per cent of the original purchase price is the usual figure.

Expenses

Each funding organisation should make clear what kind of expenses they will and will not cover. These should include the following:

- *Travel*. What class of travel will you use as the basis for your calculation? If you are including air travel, will you need fully flexible fares, or will APEX (non-refundable, non-transferable) fares be feasible? Do travel costs include local travel by taxis etc.? Do you have a set mileage rate if travel is by road? Don't forget that you may need to include the travel costs of subcontractors and participants in workshops or conferences as well as those for the project team.

- *Subsistence*. Will these be 'actuals' based on receipts from hotels and restaurants or is there an agreed per diem rate in your organisation or from the funder (there are set rates, for instance, for most EU funding programmes)? As with travel, the costs of subcontractors and workshop participants may need to be considered here.

- *Consumables*. This is a catch-all term for all kinds of things like paper and other stationery, printer toner, inter-library and document supply loan costs, charges for online database searches, etc. The usual practice is to come up with a global figure that will cover these costs for the duration of the project.

- *Costs of meetings, seminars and workshops*. For example, hiring venues, catering, etc.

VAT

This is almost always a grey area in project funding! If you pay VAT on equipment purchases and are unable to recover it easily then the costs should be included and itemised in your project costs. Most UK-based funding organisations have policies on whether they will or will not cover VAT costs on equipment and services. Projects funded by the European Commission are VAT-exempt and in theory you are supposed to be able to purchase equipment etc. free of VAT, although this is never as straightforward as it sounds in my experience. It is usually safer to assume that you will not be purchasing equipment free of VAT and to include it in your cost estimates anyway, unless the funder specifically instructs otherwise.

Risk assessment and analysis

> Risks are about the project not going to plan. They are about resources and people not being available when you want them, about machines not working, about the outputs not being of the quality you were expecting. This can happen because of an unchecked assumption, or a lack of realism in the planning, or poor organization or because you are trying to do something which is new and/or complex. If you are dependent on resources or factors outside your control the project is risky.[5]

To assess risks associated with each aspect of your project plan you need to answer the questions: 'What could go wrong, how likely is it to happen and how severe would the effects be?' You need to consider what could happen if the implementation does not go according to plan. For instance:

- Is there sufficient leeway in overcoming inevitable constraints? If it takes 5 per cent extra time to implement this activity will you still meet the deadline? If there is a price increase in this equipment procurement will you exceed the project budget?

- If you do not keep up this time schedule could it mean resources required at some later stage of implementation will not be available?

- Does the effectiveness of this activity rely upon the actions of other people and are they capable of carrying out what is required? Are they likely to meet your expectations? Are there any personal or political reasons why they may not behave as expected and required?

- Could external factors throw you off course or prevent you carrying out certain parts of the project plan?

Chapter 8 considers the nature of assumptions and risks and some techniques for analysing them.

Notes and references

1. The Fund's ICT Content Programmes: Final Evaluation Report, March 2006. See: *http://www.biglotteryfund.org.uk/er_eval_ict_final_rep.pdf*.
2. Liz MacLachlan (1996) *Making Project Management Work for You*, The Successful LIS Professional Series, ed. Sheila Pantry. London: Library Association Publishing.
3. From JISC Circular 05/06: *Learner Experiences of e-Learning*, 18 October 2006.
4. Kirsten Black (1996) *Project Management for Library and Information Service Professionals*, The Aslib Know-How Series, ed. Sylvia Webb. London: Aslib.
5. MacLachlan, op. cit.

Project planning techniques and tools

Introduction

This chapter considers, and offers guidelines on, some of the most frequently used planning techniques and tools. Useful project planning techniques and tools tend to fall into two categories:

- those that support project definition, objective setting and work planning – included here are planning methods such as objective oriented project planning, the use of the logical framework planning matrix, and risk analysis techniques;

- those that support scheduling and resources allocation – included under this category are Gantt charts for scheduling, network analysis and PERT charts.

Project management software

Project management software typically includes tools to support scheduling and resource allocation, though many producers claim that their products can support project definition as well. The range of software products – stand-alone and web-based packages – seems to increase every year. Perhaps the best known package is Microsoft (MS) Project, but there are many other, cheaper packages that offer similar types of functionality. There is a useful source of information on project management software at *TopTenReviews* from the USA,[1] where you can see annual reviews of a range of applications, with price and function comparisons.

While the software offers valuable support to scheduling – employing techniques such as Gantt charting and critical path analysis – there are, in my view, some disadvantages in relying too heavily on the software when you are planning your project.

- It is all too easy to get caught up in using the software, with the risk that its particular view of shaping a project can drive the priorities of your project rather than your views and those of other stakeholders. Don't turn to the software until you have clearly established and agreed your project objectives, required inputs and outcomes, and major work packages and tasks, using simpler techniques like pen and paper and, perhaps, an MS Excel spreadsheet!

- Many packages (including MS Project) offer complicated features to meet the needs of project management professionals, which must be understood in order to use the product effectively. Some features, such as complex task prioritisation and resource levelling, may be so complicated as to be of no use to anyone. You may easily find yourself spending more time trying to understand and make the software work than actually planning your project. For complex, multi-level projects the software packages are undoubtedly very valuable: if your project is relatively simple and straightforward they may not be worth the effort.

Techniques and tools to support project definition and objective setting

Objective oriented project planning

As discussed in Chapter 2 brainstorming your preliminary idea within a group meeting or more formal workshop is a good way of identifying the scope of a project, key aims and objectives; dependencies will become clearer and gaps in knowledge or evidence will emerge. The formal name for this kind of exercise is objective oriented project planning (OOPP). This is a participatory planning technique in which all parties involved identify and analyse the problems to be addressed in the project and prepare a concrete and realistic project plan together. OOPP brings together all stakeholders, and by discussing the problems and possible solutions the participants can come to a mutual understanding of each other's points of view. Once a form of consensus is reached these problems are organised into a logical sequence. Subsequently they are reformulated into objectives to be attained. OOPP is frequently used as an essential preliminary to the development of a formal project planning matrix (PPM) or logical framework as it is more commonly known (see below).

The typical steps in OOPP can be summarised as follows.

Steps in OOPP

Preparatory phase

- Determine the topic for the workshop (your project idea or problem to be solved).
- Identify and select all relevant parties who might have a stake in the project idea or problem.

Analysis phase

- Bring together representatives of the most relevant parties.
- Discuss the problems related to the topic.
- Build a problem tree (see below) organising the problems into cause-effect relationships.
- Build an objective tree (see below) by reformulating the problems into objectives and checking the means-ends relationships.
- Select objectives based on predetermined criteria and decide on the project focus.

Planning phase

- Prepare a project planning matrix (logical framework) using the information from the analysis phase.
- Determine means and costs.
- Draft time schedules and activities.
- Indicate the responsibilities of all parties in implementing activities.

Problem trees

Figure 8.1 is an example of a problem tree developed in a stakeholder workshop for a library development project in the Philippines.[2]

Objective tree

The objective tree developed from the problem tree in Figure 8.1 might look something like the example in Figure 8.2, with a top level, aim or purpose and a number of objectives that address the stated problems.

Figure 8.1 Example of a problem tree

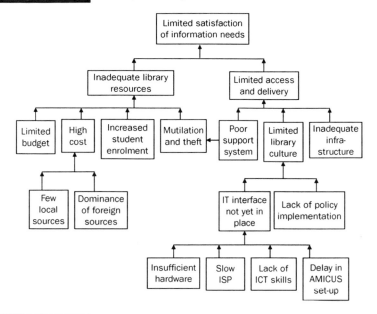

Figure 8.2 Example of an objective tree

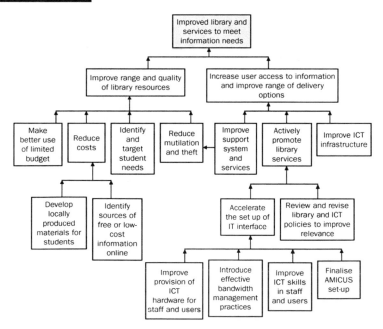

Logical frameworks

The logical framework planning matrix is used in project planning and throughout project implementation as an aid to project monitoring. Logical frameworks are commonly required in EU funding programmes (e.g. the matrix was part of the 2006 Tempus project proposal and application template), so that is a good reason to become familiar with their use. More particularly the matrix is a valuable way of organising your early-stage project plan to reveal the gaps and ensure that the whole plan hangs together in a logical and coherent manner. The logical framework will help you and your colleagues to discuss and think through all the implications of a project. Project design and planning is based on building up information and decisions and testing the links between one set of information and another. The structure of the logical framework will force your project team to:

■ identify the critical assumptions and risks that may affect the feasibility of your project; and

■ specify the indicators and evidence that will eventually be used in implementation to monitor project progress.

If you have defined the project's aims, purpose and objectives, and outputs (and outcomes) in a participatory process, it is usually the task of the designated project manager to draft a sound, logical and technically correct logical framework.

The framework is square in format and has four vertical columns and four horizontal rows and you should complete it in the order shown in Figure 8.3.

Sequence for filling in the logical framework[3]

■ The Objectives column is filled in first by working from the top to the bottom filling in boxes 1, 2 and 3. Do not fill in the 'activities' box (13) until the end.

Figure 8.3 The logical framework project planning matrix

	1 Objectives	2 Indicators	3 Evidence	4 Assumptions
Aim(s) or overall outcome	1	7	8	
Project purpose	2	9	10	6
Project outputs	3	11	12	5
Activities	13	14	15	16
			Pre-conditions	4

- The Assumptions column is filled in second by working from the bottom (preconditions) to the top (project purpose) filling in boxes 4, 5 and 6. The relationships between the objectives and the assumptions test the level of risk. The Assumptions column includes the external factors that may affect your project's outcomes but are outside your control, and tests them against the logic of the objectives.

- You then need to fill in the second and third columns (Indicators and Evidence) to establish the basis for measuring the effectiveness and clarity of the objectives. Fill in boxes 7, 8 and 9 and then 10, 11 and 12 (in order).

- Fill in the activity row (boxes 13, 14, 15 and 16) last, after you have filled in and agreed all the other components. This is to make sure that the objectives, and not the activities, lead the project. The activities are less important than the objectives and you should see them as ways of achieving the objectives.

Indicators and evidence

The last steps in drawing up a good project plan using a logical framework is formulating indicators and identifying the evidence for them. The indicators describe the aim(s), project purpose, objectives, outputs and high-level activities in verifiable terms, for instance in terms of:

- quality (the variable or element to be measured – the 'what');
- quantity (the present and future value of the variable – 'how much');
- target group ('who');
- time/period ('when');
- place ('where').

The indicators should be SMART (see Chapter 6) just as the project's objectives should be – specific, measurable, achievable/realistic, relevant, time-bound. Consider the example below:

An example of indicators

Immediate objective	'Research output in biological sciences increased through improved access to quality information services'. The indicator could be built up as follows:
Variable	Number of published research papers in biological sciences.
Target group + place	Academic staff and students in the Faculty of Science at Y University in Ourtown.
Target values	An increase of 25 per cent on current output rate.
Time	After one year.

Indicators enable verification of the viability and sustainability of the objectives and outputs, and the monitoring of progress towards their achievement (see Chapter 9). The evidence (sometimes labelled sources or means of verification) refers to the ways and places where the information can be found in order to check the indicator. These can be external sources of information or information generated within the project, which might require additional activities to be included in the project management work package.

For any evidence that lies outside the project, it should be verified at the project planning stage whether:

- its current form and presentation is manageable;

- it is specific enough;

- it is reliable;

- the costs to obtain the evidence are reasonable.

If no suitable evidence can be found then the indicators should be replaced by others. Indicators with variables that cannot be checked are of no use to the project at all!

Assumptions and pre-conditions

Assumptions are external factors, usually outside your control but which have an impact on your project performance. Assumptions can describe positive contributions such as physical resources, policy initiatives, relevance of your purpose and objectives to the attitudes of beneficiaries, etc. An example of a set of assumptions is provided below.

Example of assumptions at three different levels from Tempus project proposal of UK–Albanian Consortium

Project purpose

- Commitment to and engagement of key people in senior management and governance at the University of Tirana will be assured.

- Minstry of Education reform agenda in higher education sustains its focus on areas indicated by Albania's membership of the Bologna process, e.g. modernisation of the course structure and curriculum, stronger linkages between research and teaching, enhanced quality assurance.

Outputs and outcomes

- There is commitment to and interest in professional development among administrative and academic staff in the University of Tirana involved in graduate studies.
- Active interest exists in improving the quality of graduate studies programmes and research at the University of Tirana among graduate students and ex-alumni.
- Project consortium staff will be able to overcome any bureaucratic problems in developing new procedures and structures for graduate programme and research management that may impact on project timetables and the feasibility of objectives.

Activities

- Continuing power failures and other city infrastructure difficulties are largely overcome to avoid any serious impact on planning and implementation of project activities.
- Consortium universities will be able to field appropriate experts at appropriate times to lead workshops and undertake other expert interventions.

Not all objectives have assumptions attached and some objectives can have more than one assumption. Where assumptions concern external factors you should carefully consider their importance to the project and the realistic likelihood of your assumptions being correct. Figure 8.4 provides a useful assessment tool.[4]

Figure 8.4   Algorithm to assess external factors

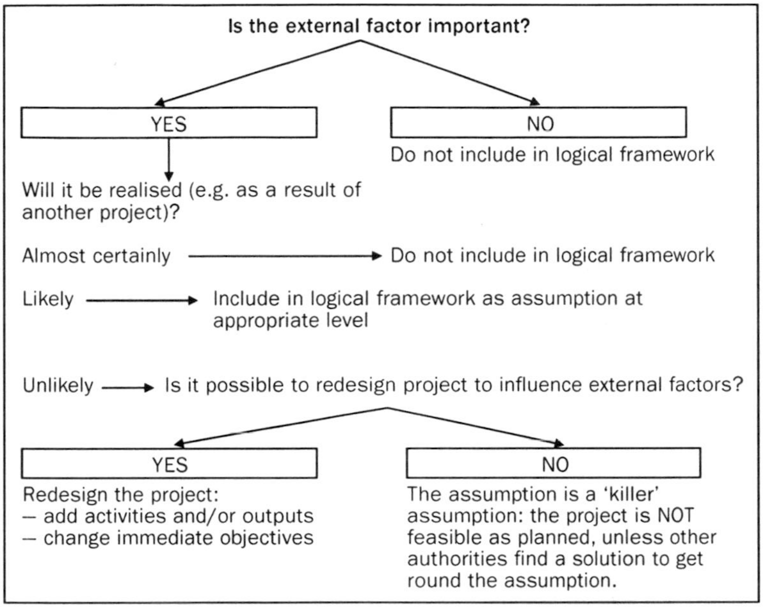

Checking the intervention logic of the logical framework

Figure 8.5 should be read as follows (from bottom to top):

- Once the preconditions are met, the activities start up.

- Once the activities have been carried out and the assumptions at this level are fulfilled, there will be outputs.

- The outputs and fulfilment of the assumptions at this level will accomplish the project purpose.

- Once the project purpose and the assumptions at this level are fulfilled the aim(s) or overall outcome will be achieved.

Figure 8.5 Intervention logic of logical framework

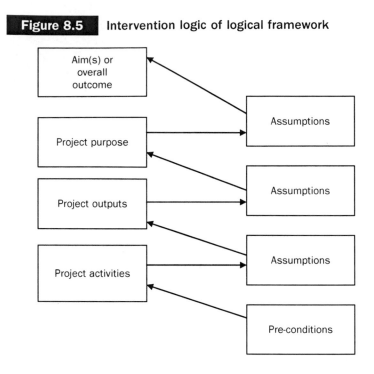

Risk checklist

Compiling a risk checklist is a useful technique for assessing the potential risks to your project and determining whether they are likely to be high, medium or low. The checklist usually comprises lists of pairs of opposing statements – one signifying low risk and the other high – with a scale between them. The items on the list will have emerged during your project planning exercise. The example in Figure 8.6, adapted from Liz MacLachlan's book,[5] shows a typical list of risk statements for each of which you would need to consider:

- where on the scale you would place your project between each low and high risk statement (allocate a number from the scale between 1 and 4, with 1 low and 4 high);

- how important each particular risk factor is to your project or what 'weight' you would assign (allocate a number between 3 and 6, with low weight 3 up to high weight 6).

These two numbers are then multiplied together to give a score for each risk and adding up the resulting scores gives the total risk score for your project. Low risk is if the total score is less than 2 × total weight (in this example that would be 62); high risk is if the total score is greater than 3 × total weight (here that would be 93). In the example in (Figure 8.6) the project is medium risk (total score = 82).

Figure 8.6 Example of a risk checklist

Low risk	Scale 1 2 3 4	High risk	Weight 3 4 5 6	Total
Full-time experienced project manager	1	Inexperienced or part-time project manager	5	5
Project team is experienced and has appropriate skills	2	Team is inexperienced and lacks some skills	3	6
Staff are dedicated to the project	3	Staff have other duties	4	12
Installation of a system which has been used elsewhere	1	Installation of a new system	3	3
Core business will not be affected	4	Project will have a significant impact on core business operations	5	20
Little constraint on completion date	4	Mandatory completion date	4	16
Suppliers are well-established and experienced	2	Suppliers are new or one-man businesses	2	4
No dependence on other projects outside manager's control	3	Heavy dependence on other projects outside manager's control	5	15
Totals	20		31	82

Tools and techniques that support scheduling and resource allocation

Gantt[6] chart

A Gantt chart is a bar chart that displays the relationship of individual work packages and main tasks to the overall timescale of the project. In its simplest form (see Figure 8.7) the time is displayed along the bottom of the bar chart and each work package is slotted into the timeline in the appropriate place. For a project timetable it is normal practice to show the main tasks of each work package on the bar chart as well. Gantt charts are widely used because they give an immediate overall impression of the project. They can be created with project management software, but also easily produced using a spreadsheet or word processor.

A Gantt chart will show clearly the maximum amount of time a project should take and those work packages that are implemented in parallel. The chart also shows what should be happening and when – if a vertical line is included for the current or a future date, it is possible to see how far the project should have got with each activity. However, it does not tell us anything about the logical interdependencies

Figure 8.7   A simple Gantt chart

	September	October	November	December
Capacity building strategy formulation				———→
Staff training needs analysis			———————→	
End user survey and interviews		———————————→		
Preparation/information gathering	——→			

between work packages and main tasks. Gantt charts can be made much more sophisticated by adding in the project milestones and, if they are based on some kind of network analysis, slack time and critical tasks.

Network analysis

Network analysis is a way of describing the flow or logic of the project, usually in a diagram that can then be analysed to show timings. Two of the most familiar network analysis techniques are critical path analysis or method (CPA or CPM) and PERT (which stands for programme evaluation and review technique). In each of these techniques the described project events, activities and non-activities are plotted to show their relationship to each other as well as to the project as a whole.

Critical path analysis

CPA breaks down a complex task into component activities to optimise performance. Any task involving more than a single operation can be analysed into sets of component activities. Success or failure of the project results from the management and scheduling of these activities. Information on likely activity durations, costs and logically necessary sequences can be used to optimise project performance.

Some activities depend on others: they can only begin when other activities have been completed. Other activities can take place concurrently. The whole project is only complete when all activities have been completed. Each activity has a duration: in CPA this is assumed to be known with certainty.

Some activities in the project will be *critical*: if these are delayed at all then the whole project is delayed. Other activities are non-critical: these can be delayed a certain amount without delaying the whole project.

This is not the place for a very detailed explanation of CPA techniques, and I am grateful to Richard Pierse from the University of Surrey[7] for the following working example of 'The Optimiser's Breakfast', which admirably demonstrates the basic principles.

Example: The Optimiser's Breakfast

Step 1: Make a list of activities, durations and precedence (if any).

Activity	Precedence	Duration
A. Get up	–	30
B. Make tea	D, E	3
C. Fill kettle	A	1
D. Fetch milk	A	1
E. Boil water	C	4
F. Milk on cereal	D	1
G. Make toast	H	4
H. Cut bread	A	2
I. Eat	B, F, G	10

Step 2: Develop a simple network that sets out the relationships amongst these activities and distinguishes *sequential* (e.g. A to C) from *concurrent* activities (e.g. C, D and H). This is the fundamental analysis, which enables a rational programme to be developed. A network diagram of the optimiser's breakfast is shown in Figure 8.8, in which *activities* are represented by arrows (labelled by letters), while *events* are represented by nodes (circles) and labelled by numbers.

Events are points in time marking the completion of activities and are represented as nodes in the network. Events are numbered serially. Thus event 0 is the node before A and event 1 is the node after A. No event can be

---

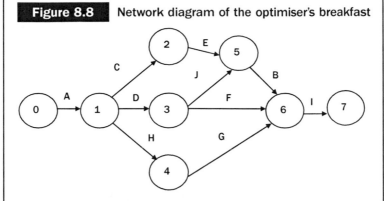

Figure 8.8   Network diagram of the optimiser's breakfast

numbered until all the preceding events have been numbered. Two nodes can be linked by at most one activity.

Dummy activities are inserted where precedence needs to be indicated but no time or other resources are consumed. For example, before tea can be made (B), water must be boiled (E) and milk fetched (D). To indicate this on the diagram a dummy activity needs to be introduced between nodes 3 and 5. This activity (J) has zero duration.

The *critical path* is the longest path of necessarily sequential activities within the project. In the example there are four paths: A–C–E–B–I, A–D–J–B–I, A–D–F–I and A–H–G–I. The problem is how to determine the lengths of the paths or the duration of the activities. For this the following concepts are useful:

- *Earliest starting and finishing times* – these are determined by a forward pass through the network. Where more than one activity ends in a node, the earliest starting time for activities *emanating* from this node is the largest earliest finishing time of the activities *ending* in the node.

- *Latest starting and finishing times* – the latest starting time for an activity is the latest time at which that activity can be started without delaying the project. The latest finishing time for an activity is the latest time that that activity can be completed without delaying the project.

Where more than one activity begins in the same node, the smaller of the latest starting times will determine the latest finishing time of activities terminating in the node.

■ *Activity slack* – is the time available for 'fine tuning' the project. On any activity it is equal to the latest finishing time minus the earliest finishing time. The critical path is the path (or paths) along which the slack on all activities is zero, i.e. it is the longest necessary path through the network.

The PERT method

PERT could be seen as a bit of a grey area. In its purest sense, it is another way of arriving at a detailed project schedule with appropriate timings; in most applications it seems to be another way of drawing the project schedule (PERT chart) with timings arrived at using the critical path method![8]

The principal difference between the PERT method and CPA is that using PERT you arrive at three different time estimates for each activity instead of a single estimate of activity duration in CPA. PERT uses a mathematical approach to establishing the project schedule.

■ O – the most optimistic estimate of time;

■ L – the most likely estimate of time;

■ P – the most pessimistic estimate.

The estimate of time will be calculated with the formula (O + [4 × L] + P)/6 (see Chapter 7 on duration of activities). Once you have established an expected time for each activity, you then analyse the network in much the same way as using CPA.

The use of project management software, such as MS Project, greatly assists the task of network analysis by automating the production of both Gantt and PERT charts using information on tasks, duration and resource allocation entered once only. The software will produce very professional-looking charts and project schedules. However, the disadvantage can be that the software is often used without project managers and teams understanding the fundamentals of network analysis that underpin PERT charts in particular, therefore allowing the software itself to drive their view of activity interdependencies and task duration, without themselves having done the essential and detailed thinking that makes a project plan really viable.

Notes and references

1. *http://project-management-software-review.toptenreviews.com/*
2. Adapted from Vlaamse Interuniversitaire Raad (VLIR)/Flemish Interuniversity Council Programme for Institutional University Cooperation (IUC): Phase II of IUC cooperation for Benguet State University, The Philippines: Appendix PP – The Library Development Project Problem Tree.
3. Adapted from 'A Project Cycle Management and Logical Framework Toolkit – A Practical Guide for Equal Development Partners', prepared by Freer Spreckley, Local Livelihoods Ltd, for the GB Equal Support Unit.
4. Adapted from 'Project Planning, Project Design and Logical Frameworks: A Guide to Objective Oriented Project Planning and Logical Framework Analysis' (and a tool for the development of project proposals) by the Management for Development Foundation/South Asia. Prepared for and with ILO-OPEC Mekong sub-regional project to combat trafficking in children and women, November 2000.

5. Liz MacLachlan (1996) *Making Project Management Work for You*, The Successful LIS Professional Series, ed. Sheila Pantry. London: Library Association Publishing.
6. Named after Henry Gantt, an American industrial engineer, who reputedly invented the charting technique in the early twentieth century.
7. Richard Pierse, Department of Economics, University of Surrey. His course notes in which this example can be found are at: *http://www.econ.surrey.ac.uk/staff/rpierse/cop1.pdf.*
8. Kirsten Black (1996) *Project Management for Library and Information Service Professionals*, The Aslib Know-How Series, ed. Sylvia Webb. London: Aslib.

9

Monitoring, evaluation and impact assessment

Introduction

The importance of effective monitoring and evaluation of project progress and outcomes is now widely recognised, and funding organisations will normally expect to see resources specifically dedicated to these tasks, as well as some assessment of potential project impact. Most practitioners reading this book will undoubtedly have experience of designing and implementing some kinds of monitoring and evaluation activities, linked to operational or project-based work.

However, despite the increasing ubiquity of such activities, many organisations and project teams omit any detailed consideration in the planning process of how their projects will be monitored and evaluated, and very often overlook the need to include such activities in their project work plan, resource allocation and scheduling. The critical point to bear in mind is that if monitoring and evaluation activities are not fully integrated into a project plan, it is then virtually impossible to undertake effective and meaningful evaluation at the end of the project.

This chapter starts by revisiting the definition and purpose of monitoring, evaluation and impact assessment to clarify the differences between the three. It then provides some practical guidelines on possible methodologies, both quantitative and qualitative, that could be employed to gather monitoring, evaluative and impact assessment information and evidence.

Definitions

Monitoring

Monitoring is the regular observation and recording of activities taking place in a project, a process of routinely gathering information on key aspects of the project in order to check on how project activities are progressing.

Monitoring usually involves giving feedback about the progress of the project to the funders and stakeholders in the project, and this reporting also enables the gathered information to be used in making decisions for improving project performance.

Monitoring typically provides the kinds of information that will help in:

- determining whether the inputs into the project are well utilised;
- identifying any problems facing the project team and finding solutions;
- determining whether the way the project was planned is the most appropriate way of solving the problem at hand;
- ensuring that all activities are carried out properly by the right people and in time.

Evaluation

In his classic text on the evaluation of social change programmes, Suchman[1] suggests five categories of criteria according to which success or failure of a programme or project may be evaluated:

- Effort – what was done?
- Performance – what were the results?
- Adequacy – how well were the real needs met?
- Efficiency – could it have been done any better?
- Process – how and why did the project work or not?

Suchman uses the analogy of the study of a bird's flight, perhaps a stage of migration. One could think of trying to establish:

- how many times it flapped its wings (effort);
- how far it flew (performance);
- how far that was in terms of the total distance it had to travel (adequacy);
- whether it could have got there quicker or with less effort by flying at a different height, taking advantage of air currents, etc. (efficiency); and
- how well its form (weight, wing span, etc.) is adapted to migratory flight (process).

Evaluation is, therefore, a process of judging the value of what a project has achieved in these terms, particularly in relation to activities planned and overall objectives. Since it involves value judgement it is different from monitoring, although it can draw on the same information gathered for monitoring purposes.

Evaluation should provide a clear picture of the extent to which the intended objectives of the activities and the project have been realised, and identify the constraints or bottlenecks that might hinder the project in achieving its objectives. Unless it is an *ex post* evaluation then solutions to the constraints can be identified and implemented. Evaluation also enables the project planners and implementers to assess the benefits and costs that accrue to the target beneficiaries (and other stakeholders) of the project.

For most funding organisations, evaluation is considered essential for drawing lessons from the project implementation experience and using those lessons in the planning of other funding programmes and projects.

Evaluation can and should be done before (*ex ante*), during (formative) and after (*ex post*) project implementation.

- Before project implementation, evaluation is used to assess the possible consequences and impact of the planned project for the target beneficiaries over a period of time, to assist in making a final decision on what project alternatives should be implemented and to assist in making decisions on how the project will be implemented.

- During project implementation, evaluation is normally undertaken at specific review points in a project, once or more times depending on the length of the project implementation period (e.g. mid-term evaluation, annual reviews). This enables the project team to review the project strategies according to the changing circumstances in order to achieve (or adjust) the activity and project objectives.

- After project implementation, evaluation is used to retrace the project planning and implementation process and to assess the final results. The evaluators will assess the actual benefits (outcomes) and the number of people who benefited, and provide ideas and conclusions on the strength of the project concept and plan.

Impact assessment

The term 'impact assessment' sums up the processes of monitoring and analysing the intended and unintended consequences, both positive and negative, of your planned project interventions, including any social change processes that may have been invoked by those interventions.

The impact of projects and their activities is often hard to predict or to anticipate. You may have started out with a broad view of what kind of impact you wanted to make on your target beneficiaries, but you may only be able to control the outputs and outcomes of your project. Your project activities may be among a much wider range of social, economic and cultural factors impacting on people's lives and experience.

The impact of any intervention usually manifests over a period of time too long to be encompassed within a project of less than two years' duration. Frequently funding organisations and project teams talk about impact assessment when what they really mean is the evaluation of project outcomes and immediate results.

Establishing indicators for monitoring and evaluation

As noted in Chapter 8, a good project plan will have formulated indicators to monitor progress towards objectives and to measure outputs and outcomes. It will have identified the evidence and sources of verification for the indicators. The indicators will show the extent to which the objectives of every activity have been achieved. Monitoring and evaluation indicators typically include:

- *input indicators*, which describe what goes on in the project (e.g. number of computers procured and amount of money spent) and are usually quantifiable and easily verifiable;

- *output indicators*, which describe the project activities (e.g. number of training workshops delivered, number of publications produced) and are also usually quantifiable and, therefore, easily verifiable;

- *outcome indicators*, which describe the results of the activity (e.g. number of library staff trained, number of publications sold) and are not always quantifiable. They may be quality indicators, relying on evidence, for instance, of increased take-up of services by different groups due to improvements in opening hours or improved methods of delivery.

Impact indicators are harder to define and verify because they are almost never directly quantifiable and almost always subjective and situational. More often than not, selected impact indicators are 'surrogate' or 'proxy' indicators that are not direct evidence, but are information from which it is possible to infer that a desired change has taken place or not. These are what you will need to look for – signs or signals – that show, by their presence or absence, whether or not the project as completed has had the desired impact. For example, if your project is an online learning project about healthy eating, and one of its aims (a desired or potential impact) was to change eating habits, one surrogate indicator of impact might be a reduction in the number of times per week the members of the target community eat meat; another might be a lively trade in vegetarian recipes within the virtual learning community set up by your project!

Choosing monitoring and evaluation methodologies

Your choice of monitoring and evaluation methodologies, when you are planning the project, will depend largely on what indicators you have set and what resources you have at the disposal of the project.

> Evaluations have to be individually designed so as to provide the greatest possible amount of directly useful information, focused and organised so as to be of the greatest value to the decision-makers [of the project being evaluated], given all the circumstances and constraints of the moment. The evaluation should also be 'good enough' to answer the practical questions being addressed, rather than necessarily 'the best', in terms of methodology; the latter could be unnecessarily demanding of resources, and could yield information in an inappropriate, even counterproductive form.[2]

In most cases you are likely to use a mix of quantitative (e.g. surveys, gathering statistical data) and qualitative (e.g. focus groups, interviews, observation) methods. The mix will allow you to gather evidence about indicators in different ways, to 'triangulate' or validate different assessment findings. Table 9.1 suggests when quantitative and qualitative approaches are appropriate in relation to project indicators.

To continue with my example above, to find out whether behaviour (for instance, eating habits) within your target community has significantly changed as a result of your online learning project, you might start, before the project begins (in an *ex ante* evaluation), by gathering information from community members in a questionnaire survey about how many times they eat meat in a week (one of your surrogate impact indicators): this will be your baseline information.

Then you might follow up with the same group and the same question after your project outputs have been available and in use for some time, by repeating the questionnaire

	Outputs (monitoring)	Outcomes (evaluation)	Impact (impact assessment)
Quantitative methods	What outputs? How many? How long? Where? When?	Take-up and use of outputs among target groups Geographical distribution/spread of use	What happened? (Quantifiable 'surrogates' or 'proxy' indicators)
Qualitative methods	Awareness of outputs among target groups Opinions about outputs among target groups	What outcomes? Quality of outcomes Who has been affected? How have they been affected?	What kinds of impact? Impact upon whom? How has the impact manifested itself?

Table 9.1 Quantitative and qualitative approaches to evaluation

survey to gather information about change since the baseline exercise. Their answers will provide information not only on whether the desired impact has happened but to what extent (proportion of target community) it happened.

On the other hand, if you want to find out whether the project outcomes have had any impact on attitudes or feelings (for instance, a different attitude towards an individual's health, or greater awareness of food issues) a discussion forum, such as a focus group, will be more effective, as feelings and attitudes are not 'quantifiable' or easily comparable across different individuals.

Both these examples point out the importance of developing an initial 'baseline' of knowledge and understanding about your target audience relevant to the areas in which you hope your project will have an impact.

Impact assessment is about measuring change and progression, so you will need to know where you came from so you can compare it to where you end up!

Including sufficient time to achieve good results in your project evaluation and impact assessment may be a challenge. Project outputs can be carefully scheduled and controlled, and project outcomes may follow immediately the outputs are delivered. For instance, if a user completes part one of your project's web-based healthy eating learning package (one of your project's outputs) there will be an immediate learning gain (outcome). The impact of that learning gain, however, may take a long time to emerge and may be subject to non-predictable influences. For instance, the learning gain in knowing more about healthy eating may only result in changed behaviour when a favourite fruit appears in the shops!

Guidelines on methodologies

This section is intended to highlight some key aspects of qualitative and quantitative research methodologies commonly used in project monitoring and evaluation, and to indicate some of the advantages and disadvantages of each method, to help you make decisions in planning your project evaluation activities. These guidelines are not intended to be comprehensive guides to methodologies.

Surveys

Surveys can be used to gather both quantitative and qualitative information. You need to be clear at the start what kind of data and evidence you want: whether it is quantitative or qualitative will have important implications for survey and sample design.

Questionnaire design

The following are useful steps in the questionnaire design process.

Before you start

- Be clear about what the objectives of the survey exercise are; this will help you to focus the research and concentrate on the questions you really need to answer. You need to ensure that the objectives of a survey are fully translated into a series of questions, which will, as far as possible, obtain the required information in an unbiased way.

- Consider data analysis before you start thinking about data collection. If you design questions in the wrong way, they will be difficult or impossible to analyse. There are a number of web-based survey and analysis packages available which can greatly facilitate the analysis task, but they need quite a lot of expertise to use them effectively.

- Consider how to make the questions meaningful to your potential respondents. If the questions seem irrelevant, confusing or misleading then you will get a low response and poor quality data. The topic of the survey may also need some preliminary explanation to survey respondents.

- Check that you are not asking questions that could be answered from existing research or other sources of information.

Question design

Questions in a survey can be 'open' (respondents are free to give any response) or 'closed' (respondents select from options provided by the interviewer). Closed questions, which require respondents to select from a number of predetermined answers, are less demanding for the respondent and much easier to analyse.

Example of a closed question

Q. In terms of paying for social care and help for older people, which of these statements is closest to your own views?

(a) The person needing the social care and help should receive money from the government/council, which they use to choose which care services they receive.

(b) The government/council should choose which social care services are provided to the person needing care and pay for them directly.

(c) Don't know.

Data from closed questions provide a sound basis for comparisons of answers across sub-groups in the sample. (For instance, are the views of people in different age groups broadly similar or not?) On the other hand, while open questions can provide richer data and the questions are less complex to construct, survey interviews generally take longer to complete and data analysis through accurate coding (see below) is time-consuming and takes considerable expertise.

The following issues in question design need to be considered.

- You need to be sure that a survey is seen as *independent*; it must be clearly *neutral* in the questions it asks.

- Questions should be phrased in a neutral way and must not steer the respondent to a particular answer.

Example

Ask 'What are your views on the proposed new library?' *not* 'Do you agree that Anytown needs a new library?'

- The sequencing of questions is important too, as you may unwittingly steer the respondent towards a particular answer.

Example

If you ask:

Q1: Do you support the municipality's efforts to encourage new employment opportunities in the Anytown area?

Q2: Do you think building a power station in the Anytown area would reduce local unemployment?

Q3: Do you support the building of a nuclear power station in the Anytown area? ...

you lead the respondent to link the building of the power station with employment opportunities. Put Q3 before Q1 and you might get a different answer.

- Questionnaires should express questions in a clear and simple way, and be understandable with as little ambiguity as possible. In general terms, a question should be interpretable in only one way.

- The layout and design of your questionnaire is important, especially for self-completion questionnaires. A confusing layout may result in respondents missing questions or unintentionally ticking the wrong answer. An attractive and clearly laid out questionnaire which is easy to follow is much more likely to be completed correctly.

- Don't ask more than one thing in the same question. Respondents may agree with one part and not the other and you will not know which part they are responding to.

> ## Example
>
> *Don't* ask 'What do you think about the performance of the current Government and the Opposition?'

- Don't include complicated qualifications – these will just confuse people and may not allow them to say what they want to.

> ## Example
>
> Say 'Do you agree or disagree with the proposal to build a new library?' then separately 'Are current bus services adequate to service the proposed centre'? *not* 'If the municipality provides more buses, do you think the library would be a good idea?'

- Avoid using too much jargon in a question. Explain any technical terms in layman's language.
- Testing or 'piloting' your questionnaire before starting the main survey fieldwork is good practice and will help iron out problems with the questionnaire.

Sample design

When undertaking any survey, it is essential that you obtain data from people that are as representative as possible of your project's target groups. Even with the perfect questionnaire (if such a thing exists), your survey data will only be useful if your respondents are typical of the target group as a whole. For this reason, an awareness of the principles of sampling is essential to the implementation of most methods of survey research.

> ## Some definitions
>
> **Population**   The group of people, items or units under investigation.
>
> **Sample**   Some members of that population from whom information is to be collected.
>
> **Sampling frame**   The list of people from which the sample is taken. It should be comprehensive, complete and up to date. Examples of a sampling frame include the Electoral Register, a postcode address file, the telephone book.

There are two broad approaches to sampling:

- *probability sampling*, including such methods as random sampling and cluster sampling, which rely on the existence of a reliable sample frame (see definitions above); and

- *non-probability sampling*, which does not require a reliable sample frame. These guidelines focus on this approach.

Purposive sampling

A purposive sample is one that is selected by the researcher subjectively. The researcher attempts to achieve the sample that appears to him/her to be representative of the population and will usually try to ensure that a range from one extreme to the other is included.

Quota sampling

Quota sampling is often used in market research. Interviewers are required to find respondents with particular characteristics, such as people of a certain age and gender. They are given a quota of particular types of people to interview and the quota is organised so that the final sample achieved in the survey should be representative of the whole population. To design quota sampling it is necessary to:

- decide on the characteristic or characteristics of which the sample is to be representative, e.g. age, gender;

- find out the distribution of this or these variables in the total population and set the quota accordingly. For example, if 20 per cent of the population is between 20 and 30 and the sample in the survey is to be 1,000 then 200 of the sample (20 per cent) will be in this age group.

Complex quotas can be developed so that several characteristics (e.g. age, sex, marital status) are used simultaneously. The main advantages of quota sampling are speed and low cost. Interviewers have to use their initiative and local knowledge in order to fill their quotas and must tactfully decline to interview people whom they approach but who turn out to be outside the quota (i.e. without the required characteristics). Interviewers tend to choose locations such as railway stations and shopping streets. The main disadvantage of quota sampling is that interviewers choose whom they wish to interview within the required quota criteria, and may therefore select those who are easiest to interview, so introducing bias into the result.

Convenience sampling

A convenience sample is used when interviewers simply approach anybody in the street who is prepared to stop. In other words, the sample comprises subjects who are simply available in a convenient way to the researcher. There is no randomness and the likelihood of bias is high. No meaningful conclusions can be drawn from the results obtained. However, this method is often the only feasible one, particularly for researchers with restricted time and resources, and can legitimately be used provided its limitations are clearly understood and stated.

Sample size and accuracy

The size of a chosen sample is less important than its *accuracy*. A properly drawn sample of fewer than 2,000 adults can give more reliable evidence about a population of many millions for election polls and other types of social research than a huge sample of a quarter of a million that is poorly drawn. Statistical tables exist which will show the degree of precision (the sampling error) which is theoretically obtainable for samples of different size.

Semi-structured interviews

A semi-structured interview is usually a face-to-face meeting between two people in which the research participant answers questions which have broadly been predetermined by the researcher, but in which the interviewer is free to pursue a line of enquiry about a particular topic that might arise from the responses to the questions. The degree of structure necessary will depend on how factual is the information sought; if detailed answers are required then it may be necessary to use probing questions to facilitate this. The objective of the research may be best met by not imposing too much structure on the participant's answers. This also means, however, that the interview is more susceptible to bias.

The semi-structured interview is typically used as:

■ a tool for obtaining particular types of information (e.g. sensitive or personal views) not easily obtained by alternative means;

- an exploratory device to help identify key issues to guide another phase of the research;

- a supplement to other methods, to follow-up, for example, unexpected results or to validate information;

- a tool for inviting children and other vulnerable groups to offer their thoughts and feelings on certain issues in a 'safe' environment;

- a tool for inviting illiterate or semi-literate people to offer their views in a less threatening way;

- a tool for inviting people from various ethnic and linguistic backgrounds to offer their views in a less standardised and less prescriptive way.

Advantages

- Information can be obtained from people who cannot read or who have difficulty understanding, concentrating or communicating.

- They permit flexibility and allow the interviewer to pursue unanticipated lines of enquiry.

- They permit probing and clarification to obtain complete and in-depth information.

- They make it possible for a rapport to be established and maintained with the research participant.

Disadvantages

- They can be time-consuming and costly.

- Sometimes the interviewer can unduly influence the responses of the participant.

- The participant may be inclined to provide rationalisations (e.g. socially desirable and logical reasons) for their views rather than the 'real' ones in order to meet perceived expectations.

- Different answers can be obtained depending on the perceived status/power of the interviewer. For example, a high-status and powerful interviewer may obtain 'favourable' responses to questions, while 'negative' responses, such as complaints or criticisms, may be obtained by a low-status interviewer who is perceived to have limited power.

- Interviewing requires skill: misdirected probing could alienate the participant.

- Responses are more difficult to record and analyse.

- Some participants may find it difficult to describe their feelings and thoughts in their own words.

Observation

Observation is often used as a method for considering behaviour, and can take the form of 'involved' or 'detached' observation. For example, in an evaluation of the quality of service provision for children with special needs within a particular health care community, the concern may be with the relationship between the style of behaviour of the carer (e.g. supporting, encouraging/inviting, reprimanding, criticising or forceful/punitive) and the reactions of the child being handled (e.g. responsive, aggressive or withdrawing). It might also be of interest to identify interactions initiated by the child and the types of reactions they invoke in the carer. In both these instances, an observation schedule will need to be developed to enable precise sampling of the behaviours that are of interest, and it would be inappropriate for the observer to be in any way 'involved' in the situation.

There are two key issues in planning an observation. The first is the production of an effective observation schedule, which provides precise indicators of the evidence being sought and a notation system for recording frequency, duration, exact form, intensity, co-occurrence and context for the behaviours of interest.

The second key issue is to prepare and obtain the cooperation and commitment of the research participants (those who are to be observed). They will need to be informed of exactly what is happening and for how long, and their trust must be gained before observations can commence.

Advantages of 'detached' observation

- With the establishment of trust and rapport the observer's presence may be taken for granted and people will become less self-conscious and behave more naturally.

- It is focused on specific behaviours and standardised and therefore likely to engender reliable evidence.

- There is no difficulty with the observer remaining 'impartial'.

Disadvantages of 'detached' observation

- The presence of the observer can lead to self-consciousness and may alter the behaviour of the participant.

- It can be difficult to derive information about the context of or reasons for a particular behaviour which makes it liable to be misunderstood.

- Time is needed to develop the observation criteria and schedule and to train the observers.

- Scheduling problems may arise.

- The timing of the observations may be inappropriate and thus the observations may be atypical.

Focus group discussion

Focus groups typically consist of 6 to 12 homogeneous individuals (i.e. individuals with specific characteristics in common, such as age, problems, disabilities) who are encouraged to interact about a particular topic. The researcher or facilitator joins the group and uses discussion and participant interaction as a way of collecting data on the topic. It is the interactions between the group members as well as those between the group and the researcher that allow data to emerge.

The normal process is to prepare a number of questions related to several aspects of the research topic under investigation. The questions must be clear and unambiguous, and the range of questions should cover all the aspects of interest to the researcher. As the group discussion proceeds questions that seem to be ineffective can be rephrased by the facilitator or other lines of enquiry arising from the discussion can be pursued.

The intention is not to obtain simple yes or no responses from participants but to address any ambiguities, obtain more detailed information and provoke a thoughtful discussion among those present about the research topic.

There are several common ways of recording the data:

- tape recording the group discussion, if agreement is obtained from all members of the group, which provides an aide-memoire;

- notes taken during the meeting are essential, but only brief notes are usually possible since the facilitator is busy listening and guiding the discussion;

- notes made immediately after the discussion are also essential, to clarify initial brief notes;

- notes taken by someone else during the discussion – by a rapporteur who is fully briefed on the topic and purpose of the session.

Advantages

- A variety of perspectives and explanations (rich data) can be obtained from a single data-gathering exercise.
- Sessions can be set up easily in pre-existing groups (e.g. care home residents).
- Participants frequently express a high degree of satisfaction with the outcomes of the focus group process.

Disadvantages

- A group can be dominated by a strong individual.
- If the membership of the group is too heterogeneous, the discussion may not develop.
- The group may pick up an appealing idea early in the session and fail to consider any alternatives as equally valid.
- Skilled management of the group is required to minimise these problems.
- The facilitator him or herself may dominate the group discussion inappropriately preventing other views to emerge.

Data analysis: coding

Qualitative research data consist primarily of text (e.g. interview transcripts, observations). For this reason analysis can be complex. Careful analysis demands that researchers consider the semantic relationships of the words used by the respondents by describing and classifying them under terminology unique to the subject under investigation. Such classification of terminology and language constructs is usually called *coding*. It is the process of analysing textual data into 'units' – the smallest pieces of information that may meaningfully stand alone, and then bringing these 'units' back together again to identify meaningful trends or patterns in the research participants' responses to questions, recorded discussions, etc.

The process of coding starts by reading the textual data and sorting the units of data (e.g. a statement, such as 'I am pleased to be here') into broad categories, and revising or adding to the categories as more data is sorted. Figure 9.1 illustrates the process.

It is advisable to begin with a simple coding scheme, based upon the main aspects of the research subject. Inevitably the codes will change, expand and collapse as more data is read, sorted and categorised.

The example below illustrates the principles and is based upon a study of information-seeking behaviour among users of a library and information service.

Figure 9.1   The process of identifying data categories

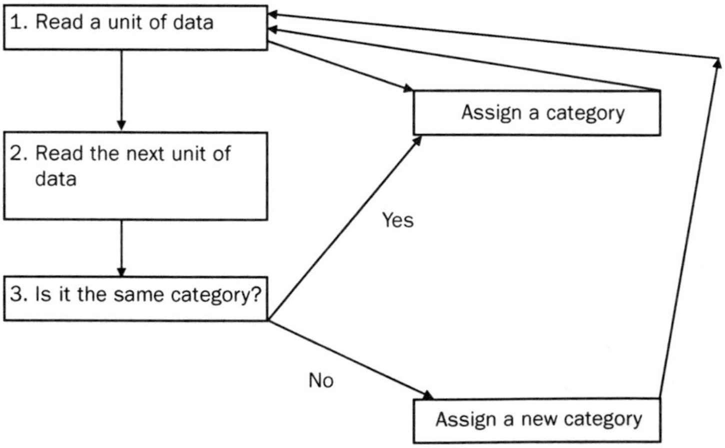

Example of qualitative data coding method

This example shows a basic coding scheme used in a study of 'information-seeking behaviour', in particular the accidental acquisition of information. The research subject area included four dimensions of information behaviour:

- the user;
- the environment;
- the information;
- the problem.

Data analysis involved coding survey and interview transcript data with the codes being developed inductively from the data.

Code term	Code definition	Supporting quotes
Exploration	The respondent was interested in knowing what information could be found in the environment. Thoughts were not concentrated on a specific task.	'I was actually exploring – just playing to see what I could find' 'Looking for anything unusual' 'What was available'
Information need	The respondent was thinking about a specific task and information needed to accomplish the task.	'Is what I was looking for available?' 'Were any of the unshelved books interesting?' 'Is the book I need among them?'
Inadequacy	The respondent's thoughts addressed a lack of confidence in the information-seeking strategy and in the skills for finding information, or dissatisfaction with the information resource itself.	'I was looking for information using a really cumbersome logic' 'I don't know so much about the World Wide Web' This book was kind of useless'

Notes and references

1. E.A. Suchman (1967) *Evaluative Research: Principles and Practice in Public Service and Social Action Programs.* New York: Russell Sage Foundation.
2. David Bawden (1990) *User-Oriented Evaluation of Information Systems and Services.* Brookfield, VT: Gower.

10

Writing effective project proposals

Introduction

Effective project proposals are those that are fit for purpose (i.e. meet the funder's requirements) and articulate a strong project rationale and plan in a persuasive manner, without overwhelming the reader with repetitive or redundant detail. Not as easy as it sounds! This chapter examines the main components of a typical project proposal and offers guidance and examples of good practice. First, however, here are two very good tips from a book by Jane Fraser,[1] which, though aimed at the commercial and marketing sector, are nonetheless valid for public sector organisations.

Identify your key competitive advantages

Your proposal can and should mention all your strengths, but it should highlight those that give you a competitive advantage. It is unrealistic to expect all your strengths to differentiate you from the competition – you may be competing with other organisations with similarly broad experience, convenient location, etc. Under these circumstances you might decide to highlight the innovative nature of your project or the outstanding track record of your project team: in other words, you may be able to identify a unique selling point (USP). Some of the things that might constitute a USP for libraries, museums and archives include:

- exceptional experience in the field – with this type of project;
- unique access to key experts;
- size, capacity and reach;
- knowledge and understanding of key target audiences.

Draw up a schedule for writing, revising and final production

The funder will probably require proposals to reach them by a certain date. Draw up a schedule for preparing your proposal to meet that deadline – and include three or four days at the end to allow for disasters. Jane Fraser says:

> Be realistic about the length of time it will take you to write the proposal. One way of estimating the writing time is to take the expected length of the proposal and express it in terms of number of words – a page of one-and-a-half line spaced text is about 350 words. Most people, if they are doing nothing else, will be able to generate no more than 2,000 words of carefully considered prose in a day. Proposal writers will probably have other calls on their time so even 1,000 words a day might be an optimistic estimate. Be conservative in your estimates and delegate early if you foresee problems.

Remember to examine your organisation's files and records for previously produced proposals from which you may be able to cut and paste relevant text, although care should be taken to make sure the final product is seamless!

Who is going to read and assess the proposal?

When writing your proposal bear in mind who is likely to be reading and assessing it. A committee of independent assessors will probably evaluate it and you should remember that they will have to read many other submissions as well. They may never read every word of your proposal, but may attempt to pick out the key points and issues they see as important, so the organisation and 'signposting' of your proposal will be crucial. They may not be native English speakers, and even if they are, keeping your language simple and direct, with short, active sentences, short paragraphs and good headings, will be a blessing for everyone!

Proposal assessment criteria

Many funding organisations will make clear how they will assess the proposals submitted and what criteria they will use. The example in Table 10.1 is taken from the EU's 7th Research and Innovation Framework Work Programme, and shows the three main criteria applied to different kinds of project proposal.

Sometimes funding organisations may also provide a weighting to the different criteria which will give you an indication of what sections of the proposal you should prioritise for your particular attention.

Structuring the proposal

Proposals come in many shapes and sizes and often the funders have very specific rules and guidelines on how they

Table 10.1 Example of assessment criteria from EU FP7 Work Programme

	1. Scientific and/or technological excellence (relevant to topics addressed in the call)	2. Quality and efficiency of the implementation and the management	3. The potential impact through the development, dissemination and use of project results
All funding schemes	Soundness of concept and quality of objectives	Appropriateness of the management structure and procedures Quality and relevant experience of the individual participants	Contribution at the European (and/or international) level to the expected impacts listed in the work programme under relevant topic/activity
Collaborative projects	Progress beyond state-of-the-art Quality and effectiveness of the S/T methodology and associated work plan	Quality of the consortium as a whole (including complementarity and balance) Appropriateness of the allocation and justification of the resources to be committed	Appropriateness of measures for the dissemination and/or exploitation of project results, and management of intellectual property
Networks of Excellence	Contribution to long-term integration of high quality S/T research Quality and effectiveness of the joint programme of activities and associated work plan	Quality of the consortium as a whole (including ability to tackle fragmentation of the research field and commitment to deep and durable integration) Adequacy of resources for successfully carrying out the joint programme of activities	Appropriateness of measures for spreading excellence, exploiting results and disseminating knowledge through engagement with stakeholders and the public at large

should be structured, providing templates with the tender or call documents (e.g. JISC). These guidelines are likely to include section headings, number of pages, point size for the type, mandatory accompanying documentation and number of copies required for submission.

Most EU funding programmes, including those under the 7th Framework Programme, Tempus and Grundtvig, now require proposals to be submitted using the Electronic Proposal Submission Service (EPSS).[2] It is advisable to become thoroughly acquainted with the structure they require in EPSS before you start to organise your work and structure your proposal.

While some funding organisations and programmes may invite pre-proposals or pre-qualification statements, all eventually are likely to require a fully comprehensive proposal. Unless you are submitting a proposal to a funder that has already provided support to your organisation in the past it is important to remember that the funder and its appraisal committee members will know nothing about your organisation at all. The purpose of the proposal is to answer all the questions that the funder might possibly want to ask you, so structuring the proposal in a logical and helpful way and being fully comprehensive (without being repetitive!) are important. Table 10.2 shows a typical structure[3] and each major section is considered in more detail below.

Executive summary

The summary is one of the most important parts of the proposal because most people will read the summary first, and some important decision-makers and influencers may read only the summary. You will be able to write the

| Table 10.2 | Typical structure for a comprehensive proposal |

Funding organisation questions	Sections in the proposal that provide the answers
What's this proposal all about and how do I find my way around it?	Covering letter Title page Table of contents Executive summary
Why are you proposing and for what?	Introduction Background or contextual statement Understanding the terms of reference (if appropriate) or Rationale (understanding the need)
What will this project do?	Approach (to the specified work) if appropriate Methodology Project work plan
How long will it take and how much will it cost?	Timetable, Gantt and PERT charts Schedule of costs
How can I be certain my money will be well spent?	Risks and assumptions Management and quality issues
Why choose to fund this proposed project and not one submitted by other organisations?	Organisation credentials and capability Personnel
Any other information?	Appendices

summary only after you have completed a first draft of the whole proposal. The summary should include:

- your name, organisational address, title of the project proposal and for whom, which programme or in response to which call for proposals it was prepared;
- a summary of the need the project sets out to address;
- how the proposed project will meet that need;
- why the funder should choose your organisation or project partnership, summarising your strengths and USP.

The summary may also include a statement of overall costs, and some funders require it (e.g. JISC), although there is a risk attached to this as the funder may dismiss the costs as excessive and never progress beyond reading the summary.

The length of a summary should normally be in proportion to the length of the proposal – according to Jane Fraser[4] about 5–10 per cent is a good rule of thumb, so a typical proposal of 20 pages or less should have a summary of no more than one page of A4.

Introduction

If your proposal is likely to be read by people whom you have never met before and who have had no prior dealings with your organisation or project partnership, then it is a good idea to introduce yourself and your project partners by stating who you are and what kinds of organisations you are, and giving one or two examples of your work and experience.

You might also use the introduction to explain briefly how the proposal is structured and what you have included in any appendices, and to ensure that your full contact details are presented – as in the example given below.

Contextual statement

To support your project proposal you may wish to begin with a brief overview of the context in which your project will be implemented, covering issues such as:

- the policy context;
- major research findings or other programme developments;
- socio-economic factors that influence developments;
- technology issues or trends.

Example: Introduction to proposal to undertake an evaluation of the New Opportunities Fund ICT Content Programmes

Introduction

Education for Change Ltd (EfC) is pleased to submit our proposal for this evaluation of the New Opportunities Fund's ICT Content Programmes in response to the letter of invitation to tender dated 27 October 2003. We believe EfC can offer an informed and effective team for this important evaluation project, based on our:

- knowledge and understanding of the wider policy context of the museums, archives and libraries domains throughout the UK;
- experience in designing and implementing evaluation research;
- professional facilitation of focus groups and round-table consultation sessions;
- expertise in drawing conclusions and making pertinent recommendations based on sound analysis and understanding of evidence and data gathered.

This Technical Proposal outlines our understanding of the policy context, our preferred evaluation methodology, and our proposed approach and methodology for the evaluation in line with the Technical Questionnaire provided in the ITT, including a work plan and timetable. It also describes the background and experience of the company and the project team.

The Technical Proposal is accompanied by a separate Commercial Proposal providing the appropriate pricing schedule and information about the company structure and finances, in line with the specification in the ITT documents.

Enquiries and further correspondence concerning this proposal should be addressed to [etc.].

For some funding programmes, such as the EU programmes, this kind of context-setting statement is essential to establish you and your partners' knowledge and awareness of important trends and developments in the specific field of the project.

Example: Contextual statement from proposal to undertake an evaluation of the New Opportunities Fund ICT Content Programmes

The policy context of the NOF's ICT Content Programmes

This evaluation of NOF's ICT Content Programmes must be set in the context of cultural, social and economic policy in the UK as a whole and the evolving policies of devolved government in Scotland, Wales and Northern Ireland as well as the English regions. The policy and funding context is dynamic and much has changed since the inception of the NOF Programmes in 1999.

Government policies in Cultural Heritage

In 1998 the Department for Culture, Media and Sport (DCMS) published an important and formative review of the structure and funding of the arts and cultural sector in the UK – *A New Cultural Framework* – in the context of the Department's own Spending Review. This review was intended 'to establish a new role for DCMS, giving it a more strategic place in the complicated structures of cultural policy and funding [and] to announce a new relationship between [DCMS] and the bodies [it] fund[s] to ensure the delivery of appropriate outputs and benefits to the public.' The review noted 'in all cases the financial

---

allocations will be closely tied to outcomes which reflect [DCMS's] four central themes: access, excellence and innovation, education and the creative industries.'

Developments such as ICT networking, the emphasis on lifelong learning and moves towards greater coordination of public services induced DCMS to reappraise the services delivered by the full range of cultural institutions for which it is responsible. A number of key policy documents, such as *Libraries for All: Social Inclusion in Public Libraries* and *A Common Wealth: Museums in the Learning Age* set the policy agenda. At the same time DCMS announced its intention to wind up both the Libraries and Information Commission and the Museums and Galleries Commission (MGC) and set up an entirely new body, Resource: the Council for Museums, Archives and Libraries, which came into being in 2000.

The DCMS review was influential in Scotland, where the Scottish Executive published *The National Cultural Strategy* in August 2000, which set out four strategic objectives, one of which was to 'realise culture's potential contribution to education, promoting inclusion and enhancing people's quality of life'.

Lifelong learning and community development

The Department for Education and Skills (DfES) has been influential in driving forward a policy of greater inclusiveness in planning and developing community skills and lifelong learning initiatives at the national and local levels, working with formal and non-formal education and training providers in the Association of Learning Providers (ALP), for instance, and the National Institute of Adult Continuing Education, as the leading non-governmental organisation for adult learning in England and Wales. The regional and local Learning and Skills Councils and regional and local government agencies have also provided significant funding for community initiatives, using ICT networking, to widen learning access, opportunity and participation.

Museums, libraries, galleries, archives, arts organisations and the built and historic environments are now understood to be educational resources for people of all ages and backgrounds, with the potential to engage adult learners with basic skills needs who do not find formal education attractive or accessible. Partnerships with formal education institutions, such as further education colleges and community schools, are also designed to integrate museums, libraries and archives more fully into the formal curriculum and to play a part in widening participation in formal education initiatives.

Under the auspices of the Social Exclusion Unit, set up to help improve government action to reduce social exclusion by producing 'joined-up solutions to joined-up problems', the DCMS embraced an increased commitment to arts and culture in neighbourhood renewal and community development, using such strategies as Internet access in public libraries, the distribution of National Lottery funding and Creative Partnerships to narrow the gap between deprived neighbourhoods and the rest of the country and improve quality of life.

Understanding the terms of reference

If you are bidding to deliver a project in which the terms of reference have already been defined by the funder (or the client) then this section provides you with an opportunity to show that you understand and can interpret those terms of reference (TOR) and, if appropriate, to make any comments on them or additions to them. Simply repeating the terms of reference word for word here will not do and would be likely to be detrimental to your proposal.

Example: Understanding the TOR in a proposal for a HEFCE-funded research study into researchers' use of libraries and other information sources

Our understanding of the terms of reference

We understand from the brief that the stakeholders in the new Research Libraries Strategy Group wish to achieve 'a suitably detailed map of the various kinds of stored information UK researchers need to access, and of the ways in which they utilise this information'. Specifically, this study will:

1. Profile the information sources, required by researchers in different disciplines, in terms of nature, range and volume.

2. Profile the nature or type of access requirements for these sources, including on-line access to research materials with its perceived advantages and shortcomings and the relative significance of the Internet as a research tool.

3. Profile the nature of the use made of these information sources.

4. Investigate the implications for research of the physical location of materials.

For all the above, the study will investigate, identify and analyse evidence of patterns and probable changes and trends over the next ten years, and will analyse the variations in requirements and practice between identifiable sub-groups of the research population, including academic disciplines.

Ultimately, through the above, a baseline of well-documented and transferable evidence and recommendations will be established to underpin and guide the development and management of a distributed national research information collection and the work of the Research Libraries Strategy Group in general.

Rationale

Where specific terms of reference have not been provided, in this section your proposal should establish the rationale for your project and your understanding, based on evidence, of the need to be addressed by your project. This section tells the potential funder that you have:

- identified a specific and legitimate need or set of needs;
- researched and gathered evidence of need within specific population groups or among target beneficiaries;
- understood the steps necessary to address the problem;
- proposed specific ways of addressing the identified needs through your project.

The rationale should refer back to and take its starting point from your earlier background or contextual statement, so that links to policies, trends or recent developments are clearly defined. You may also need to support your rationale with hard evidence obtained from your research and evidence gathering undertaken as preparation for your project planning. This may take the form of statistics, charts or reference to published research, and supporting data from your own research can be included in the appendices of your proposal. Your rationale should conclude with a statement of the overall purpose or aim of your project.

Example: The rationale for the draft ERPANET project proposal

Rationale

Archives of all kinds, libraries and museums keep digital objects of cultural and scientific significance that are worth

---

preserving over time. At the moment of creation of such objects, however, preservation requirements are rarely taken into consideration. In a variety of research programmes, academic institutions, companies (e.g. pharmaceuticals) and curators are currently seeking reliable solutions to the long-term preservation of the digital heritage. Two examples of many similar projects are the European Union-sponsored NedLib project and the United States' National Archives and Records Administration (NARA) support for the work at the San Diego Computer Center.

As research continues, various scientific and cultural institutions are in the process of implementing programmes on digitising analogue materials and, subsequently, on the preservation of digitised and born-digital objects. Although in some cases these institutions cooperate and share experiences in this work, in many other cases they work in isolation and are unable to benefit from the results of current research or from the experiences arising from the day-to-day practice of institutions within the same country. This problem is even more critical across European national frontiers and across the traditional domains of libraries, archives and museums. As a consequence, there are widely differing levels of knowledge and expertise across these domains and few mechanisms in place to enable the smoother flow and assimilation of that knowledge.

To a certain extent, digitisation can be said to blur the borders between the domains, easily crossing national, linguistic and professional boundaries. Whether it is an archival document, a scientific text, a musical score or a picture, in digital format they are all just bit-streams that a preserver must be able to re-present in their original format and behaviour. As a concrete example, archival institutions and museums may benefit from the knowledge amassed on managing digital libraries, whereas libraries may learn much from the archival community about authenticity.

The ERPANET project aims to establish an expandable European Network of Excellence, which will serve as a virtual clearing-house and knowledge-base in the area of preservation of cultural heritage and scientific digital objects.

ERPANET aims to bring together in a Network of Excellence memory organisations (museums, archives and libraries), the ICT and software industry, research institutions, education, government and local government organisations, the entertainment and creative industries (e.g. broadcasting and the performing arts) and commercial institutions (including financial and petrochemical sectors, for example). The Network Contractors and members together will be representative of these disciplines in the European Union and the wider European context. The dominant feature of the ERPANET Network will be the exchanging of knowledge on state-of-the-art developments in digital preservation and the transfer of expertise among individuals and institutions. In general the Network will enable the communication and exchange of ideas among its members. More specifically the Network will deliver a range of services (e.g. content advisory service, training and expert seminars), both to members and non-members.

Approach

This section outlines your particular approach to undertaking specified research or work (where the terms of reference have been set by the client or funder) and is important in order to distinguish and differentiate your proposal from those of other bidders for the same contract. Here you should explain what is unique in the way your organisation or partnership will approach the work. This may be in terms of, for instance:

- working within a particular set of values or principles;
- using external resources accessible to you and your partners, such as willing research respondents from target beneficiary groups;

- deploying particular kinds of expertise;

- using unique kinds of research tools and/or methodology;

- drawing on a unique perspective or previous experience that is directly relevant to the topic of the proposal.

Example: Proposal to undertake an evaluation of the New Opportunities Fund ICT Content Programmes

Our approach to the evaluation

The evaluation of the two NOF Programmes, Digi and CGfL, will be a complex undertaking, given the very wide diversity of projects in terms of size of funding and organisation, kinds of project partners, national contexts, objectives and outcomes. Our approach will be to focus on what is achievable within the budgetary constraints, using rigorous and proven evaluation techniques to provide evidence to meet NOF's requirements.

Aspects of our proposed methodology will be 'scaleable' – e.g. scope of consultation could be widened, number of focus groups increased, number of case studies increased. If additional funds become available, these activities can be scaled up to focus on areas where available evidence might not be sufficiently rich to turn speculations into robust conclusions and generalisations, for instance on what makes best practice.

To assist the project team in validating outcomes throughout the evaluation period, we propose to establish a panel of 'Critical Friends', composed of key informants from the cultural heritage and education sectors, who are capable of bringing their knowledge of policy and practice to findings and in exploration of key issues with the project team. This panel will be an informal group, communicating with the project team mostly by e-mail and telephone.

> Our approach to the work will have three foundations:
>
> - an evaluation framework within which to organise a common approach to the enquiry;
> - a robust typology of projects to facilitate analysis and generalisation of evaluation outcomes; and
> - impact assessment focused principally on learning outcomes, building on tried and tested approaches.

Methodology

This is the heart of the proposal where you convince a potential funder that your proposal is a rational, practical and effective response to the need that has been identified. In my experience it is a good idea to write this section and the work plan first since everything you say in other sections will need to be informed by these or refer to them in some way, and certainly will need to be consistent with the methodology that you outline here.

The section should start with a statement of your project objectives, which could be embellished with detail of how each objective will be achieved – as in the example below from the draft ERPANET proposal.

Example: from the methodology statement from the draft ERPANET proposal

Project objectives

1. To identify and raise awareness of sources of information about the preservation of digital objects across the broad spectrum of national and regional cultural and scientific heritage activity in Europe.

The Network will identify and track those sources, provide a gateway for easy access and contribute to the development of a critical mass of information for practitioners.

2. To appraise and evaluate information sources and documented developments in digital preservation on behalf of Network Members, and to make available results of research, projects and best practice.

Not all sources are equally important or relevant for a particular project. No institution is able to appraise all the emerging information about the subject. In the Network, Contractors and Members will be able to divide the workload, and share the outcomes.

3. To provide an enquiry and advisory service on digital preservation issues, practice, technology and developments.

In many cases institutions have particular concrete questions on which they need a prompt and precise answer without knowing currently to whom to turn for answers and advice. The Network will serve as a direct knowledge-base, as well as a clearing-house to respond to such questions and the answers to which will contribute to the growing knowledge-base.

4. To implement a suite of six development seminars to bring together experts from a range of disciplines to address key preservation issues (e.g. integrity and audit requirements, emulation and migration).

The Network will disseminate the results widely for the benefit of Network Members and non-members. The seminars will be three-day discussion meetings. Each will be organised in different European regions to maximise their impact and demonstrate commitment to wide dissemination of the Network outputs and increase the sense of community ownership of ERPANET.

5. To build a suite of eight training workshops based on best practice (in such areas as building e-records procedures and policies, preservation of e-mail and web materials), and to identify where and what further practitioner training and staff development is required.

Few practising librarians, archivists and curators possess a sufficiently substantial body of knowledge about the technology and management issues they have to deal with in digital preservation. The training workshops will be two-day events, organised by the Contractors in their regions to ensure Europe-wide participation, with materials developed for the workshop and then made freely available to the community at the ERPANET website for use by others, as well as to enable those who took part in the training sessions to share their new knowledge with colleagues in their home institution.

6. To develop a suite of tools, guidelines, templates for prototype instruments and best-practice case studies.

Research results have to be transformed into practical guidelines or tools, and best practice clearly identified. The Network will make significant contributions to the available corpus of work on digital preservation and ensure that a growing databank of material is available to meet a variety of information, training and awareness-raising needs across a range of European cultural, linguistic and technological contexts. The tools will meet the needs of SMEs and smaller memory organisations by providing them with clear and easily implementable guidelines to enable them to address their preservation challenges.

7. To stimulate further research on digital preservation in key areas and encourage the development of standards where gaps and opportunities have been identified.

Technology is continuously changing and consequently new research questions will arise. The Networks will promote research and formulate appropriate research questions. In spite of the fact that the standardisation community is most active in developing norms, guidelines and standards, still much work has to be done. The Network will help to define where standards may contribute in solving problems or where members might act together to enable (and support) new research.

In the Methodology section you need to explain broadly how you are going to tackle the work you propose, for instance:

- what key stages you see involved (e.g. feasibility, development, testing and appraisal);
- what research methodologies you intend to use and why (e.g. desk research, focus groups, questionnaire survey);
- what special resources or tools you intend to employ (e.g. subcontracting technical specialists, developing specific research or analytical tools).

You can go into considerable detail to support your main points and include consideration of alternative methodologies and why you have decided not to use them if this is appropriate, as illustrated in the following example from a proposal to the ESRC and British Library.

Example: Methodology statement from a study proposal submitted to the ESRC and the British Library

We have designed a project based on four principal elements:

- initial preparation;
- sample design and identification;

- intensive exploration of collections, services and needs;
- extensive consultation with the research community.

Initial preparation

This first stage will require consultation and dialogue with the British Library and the ESRC. On the one hand we will need to make an assessment of collections in key areas – strengths, nature and extent of the collection. We will also need to gather data on existing use of relevant collections. Thirdly we will need to be sure that we understand the BL's aspirations for their social science collections as well as their current efforts and plans to promote and increase their use.

On the other hand, we will need to agree the scope of the investigation – the range and nature of the social science community to be covered, key subject areas – with ESRC stakeholders and to understand the range of possible activities/programmes that the ESRC might consider in relation to exploiting BL collections more effectively on behalf of key groups in its community.

Sample design and identification

At this initial stage we will also identify the population from which we can select the research samples that will be used for both the intensive exploration and the extensive consultation. Named individuals will be identified through consultation, searches of institutional websites and more general Internet searches. We also hope that we will be able to draw on records of ESRC awards to help with this process. This will enable us to be more structured when selecting participants for the intensive exploration stage and it will enhance the reliability and rigour of the survey outcomes.

Intensive exploration of collections, services and needs

We recognise that most social science researchers will have an incomplete understanding of the scope and nature of the

British Library's collections. Many will be familiar with certain parts of the collection but few will have an overall appreciation of what the Library holds and what it can offer. Without an understanding of the full scope and nature of the collection, it will be hard for researchers to identify what they are failing to utilise and, more particularly, how the collection and services could be made more relevant and accessible.

We believe that the scope of the British Library's collection relevant to population change and globalisation is so broad that the most effective way of achieving an understanding of what the British Library has to offer to the social science research community is through offering small groups of researchers the opportunity to visit the Library, to explore the collections and services directly and to meet the staff who work with the collections. The aim would be to create a situation in which researchers can have an informed, in-depth discussion of the strengths of the collections and the ways in which their accessibility and range might be improved.

We propose to select three groups of 12–15 researchers, all of whom work in the specific areas of population change or globalisation within the London/M25 area to keep travel constraints to a minimum and maximise attendance: one group of established academics, one group of postgraduate students and a third group of non-academic (government and/or private sector) researchers. Each will be invited to a one-day workshop at the British Library. During the morning they will be given a thorough introduction to the collections and services on offer, by the end of which they should have developed a sound understanding of the scope and nature of what is on offer. The afternoon will consist of a more general discussion of the collections, strengths, perceived gaps and areas where the collections might be extended. This will conclude with a session to identify the barriers that prevent researchers from making full use of the collections. Clearly, we will need to call on the close cooperation of the BL staff when designing and running these workshops.

Extensive consultation with the research community

The intensive workshops will provide an in-depth picture of the strengths of the collections and services, the ways in which they could be extended and the barriers that constrain use. However, it will be a picture drawn from only a small, localised sub-set of the research community. To validate the results and to gather related evidence from the wider social science community throughout the United Kingdom, we will undertake an extensive consultation exercise.

We aim to survey a sample of researchers drawn from the population identified in the initial preparation stage. The size of the survey research sample will be not less than 400 individuals and we anticipate being able to achieve at least a 50 per cent response. Individuals will receive a personalised e-mail inviting them to take part in the on-line survey.

Alternatively, and especially if page restrictions for the length of your proposal have been imposed by the potential funder, you may choose to keep your statement of methodology short and rely on the work plan to provide the requisite level of detail. The ERPANET example below illustrates this approach.

Example: Overall methodology statement from the ERPANET proposal (2001)

ERPANET brings together a wide range of public sector, academic, research, industrial and commercial organisations in a virtual Network focused on the preservation of digital objects. Key aspects of the Consortium's overall methodology include:

- web-based services to facilitate information capture, delivery, coordination of activities, sharing and transfer of knowledge;

- designation of four European Zones (see C5) for which the four Consortium Contractors will be designated Content Editors and Project Enablers, responsible for identifying, evaluating and disseminating around the whole Network key documentation, research, evidence of best practice and regional/local expertise from each Zone. The Network will be multilingual;

- development of a 'critical mass' of mediated content and information on digital preservation issues and provision of facilities and services to Members and non-members to exploit this information, through dissemination activities, seminars and training workshops;

- exploiting the combined and collective knowledge, expertise and research of ERPANET Consortium and Members to build toolkits, establish guidelines and generate templates to facilitate sharing of knowledge and best practice.

While the bulk of the work will be conducted by the Network Contractors the project aims to ensure that Members make an active contribution to the process of content creation for every aspect of the project.

Project work plan

The content and length of the project work plan will vary widely among different projects, but a work plan should always answer the following questions about the project:

- What are you going to do?
- How are you going to do it?
- What will be achieved (deliverables)?
- Who will implement each part of the project?

- What resources will be needed for each part of the project?
- Where will each part of the project take place?
- When will each step of the project happen?

It is common practice to present the work plan in a schematic or tabular way, rather than a straightforward narrative, as the examples in Chapter 7 on project planning show. The important thing to check is that the work plan and narrative section on methodology are consistent with each other rather than contradictory or confusing, and that they complement each other without too much repetition. It can also be very useful, in a complex project, to make clear exactly how each part of the work plan relates to the achievement of the project's objectives. This can be done as a simple schematic, as in Figure 10.1 below.

Timetable

Your timetable should be a chart that is readable and understandable at a glance. This can be more difficult in longer, complex projects and you may need to split your

Figure 10.1 From draft ERPANET proposal – objectives and related work packages

Objective 1	Objective 2	Objective 3	Objective 4	Objective 5	Objective 6	Objective 7	Objective 8	Objective 9
WP1	WP1	WP1	WP1	WP1	WP1	WP1	WP1	WP1
WP3	WP2	WP4	WP5	WP6	WP2	WP3	WP7	WP4
	WP3	WP7	WP7	WP7	WP4			WP6
	WP4				WP7			

schedule up by date periods (e.g. Year 1, Year 2). In the timetable you need to give the potential funder an overview of when each part of the project will happen, for how long and when the particularly critical points (milestones) in the project will be reached. Unless the funder has specified more detailed requirements for the time schedule, in my experience it is best to keep the details to a minimum.

Whether you use a Gantt chart generated by project management software (see Chapter 8) or whether you create your own chart or table in Word or Excel you may help the reader by highlighting key steps or key components in colour. If your project is an international one, you may wish to indicate through colour coding or shading which stages or activities take place in the field or in the UK, for instance.

Schedule of costs

Most funders specify how they wish to have the costs presented and broken down – consider the budget template from a Big Lottery Fund application form in Figure 10.2.

The schedule of costs should be consistent with the details of effort (number of person-days) that you might have included in the work plan. It should also be clear about whether or not it includes VAT costs, where these are appropriate. If your project is very complex the potential funder will be grateful for the inclusion of a summary of the main costs and the total costs, either in a narrative introduction to your cost schedule or in the project summary itself.

Risks and assumptions

Every project entails risks and involves a number of assumptions that may or may not turn out to be accurate.

Figure 10.2 Big Lottery Fund application form: budget template

3.5 Project Budget

Complete the following table to show us how much the project will cost and what you will spend the grant on.

Please note that 'Year 1' is the 12 month period from our offer of grant to you:

	Total project costs – include VAT where applicable					Total	VAT recoverable from total	Funding from other sources	Amount requested from Big Lottery Fund
	Year 1	Year 2	Year 3	Year 4	Year 5	A	B	C	A – B – C
Direct revenue costs									
Total direct revenue costs									
Direct capital costs									
Total direct capital costs									
Overheads									
Total overheads									
Total project costs									

If you are asking us to fund overheads, what percentage of your organisation's total overheads does this represent?   %

You will have identified these risks and assumptions during the project planning phase (see Chapter 7) and you will need to summarise the main ones in your presentation and show how you intend to mitigate the risks or overcome them. It is essential that you do show the funder that you have identified and faced up to potential risks and problems, and that you have clear contingency plans in place. Very common among project risks are:

- slippage in the time schedule;
- costs exceeding budgets;
- personnel changes that impact on implementation or management;
- policy or strategic changes within parent organisations that impact on the project;
- project management problems if the partnership is large and not very cohesive.

Example: Risk assessment in a feasibility study for VLIR-UOS

Risk	Assessment	Mitigating actions
Reluctance of some key informants to cooperate fully where there are vested interests or concerns	High	We will seek opportunities to accommodate and reflect interests of various actors We will also seek support from VLIR-UOS to emphasise the importance it attaches to the work

---

Risk	Assessment	Mitigating actions
Difficulty making appointments, contacts and collecting evidence in country field missions	Medium	Clarify with VLIR-UOS what support can be expected from the local partner programme coordinators Agree on field visit countries in sufficient time to allow for adequate preparation Make use of EfC and South Research contacts in-country where these exist to collect background information
Time constraints on completion of evaluation work may impact on quality of outcomes	Medium	Ensure early dialogue and document acquisition with VLIR-UOS Clarify flexibility in start and end dates for the work Where appropriate run field missions in countries where EfC evaluators are already scheduled to visit in order to exploit administrative efficiencies

Management and quality issues

Project management

If the project has a number of different partners with different roles, it is a good idea to include a statement on how the project will be managed, covering some or all of the following kinds of points:

- whether there will be a project board, its composition and powers;

- who will be responsible for the day-to-day management and administration, and a brief statement of their experience;
- who will be responsible for project reporting and financial matters;
- what the main communication and decision-making channels will be, e.g. how project partners will meet and when, whether there will be a discussion forum or ftp site set up for exchange of ideas and circulation of documents, etc.

Quality

If you have a quality policy or strategy in your organisation then refer to it and quote from it here; or if your organisation is accredited with, for instance, ISO 9000 or Investors in People, make a statement about that here.

Organisational credentials and capability

Capability statement

Some organisations prefer to put this section right at the front of the proposal, and there are pros and cons to each approach. Essentially, however, this is the section that needs to show that your organisation, partners and project team are up to the job that has been set and, in my view, it makes sense to include details of organisational capacity, people and references to past experience after you have described and presented the job (project) in question.

An organisational capability statement will include:

- a statement about the broad nature of the organisation – when it was established, how large it is in terms of staff, catchment area, turnover, etc., its main areas of business, mission, values and purpose;

- an indication of past and current experience – project or operational work – that is relevant to the nature of the project being proposed; this can take the form of summaries of past projects or main work areas.

Example: Capability statement from Education for Change Ltd

Education for Change Ltd (EfC) specialises in consulting, research and project management for education and information development and also works in cultural heritage and other social sectors. EfC was formed in 1992 as a partnership of consultants and became a limited company in 1997. We have offices in central London and seven staff, from different countries and professional backgrounds, and a small number of closely associated consultants.

EfC has experience of managing complex and multi-country evaluations based on shared evaluation frameworks. We have extensive experience both of qualitative and participatory methods to determine the perspectives of beneficiaries and stakeholders and of collecting evidence from policy-makers, institutions, operational managers and staff.

EfC has an active portfolio in the UK, in the developing countries of Africa and Asia and in the transitional economies of Europe and Central Asia. Major clients include the UK's Department for International Development (DFID), the World Bank, the Asian Development Bank, UNESCO and a range of public sector organisations within the UK, including the Higher Education Funding Councils and their Joint Information Systems Committee (JISC). Recent and relevant projects and major contracts undertaken include the following:

- In association with the University of East London, EfC has recently (2006) completed work in the UK on a study of Strategies for Managing ICT and Its Applications within Colleges and Universities: Policy and Practice, one of several studies under the JISC Management and

---

Leadership Programme. EfC provided consulting and research support.

- EfC has recently (2006) completed the Evaluation of the Mediterranean Virtual University project. The Mediterranean Virtual University is a €4m project, funded under the European Commission's European Mediterranean Information Society (EUMEDIS) Programme, led by the University of Strathclyde with partners in Malta, Cyprus, Egypt, Palestine, Jordan, Lebanon, Turkey and Denmark. EfC provided consultants as external evaluators to the project.

- EfC is currently providing evaluation expertise to the Knowledge Economy Project under the Ministry of Communications and Information Technology in Romania (funded by the World Bank). The project aims to support knowledge-driven activities at the national level as well as directly within local communities and, in particular, to accelerate the participation of disadvantaged communities in the knowledge economy and society. EfC and local partners assist the project management unit (PMU) in assessing the project interventions related to access to information on the selected communities.

- EfC recently completed (2006) a two-year Evaluation of the Big Lottery Fund ICT Content Programmes that supported community development and lifelong learning in the UK: over 200 projects in the Digitisation Programme (grants totalling £50 million) and the Community Grids for Learning Programme (£5 million) created digital content relevant to cultural heritage, social inclusion, civil renewal and environmental awareness.

- In 2005, EfC undertook the evaluation of the role of UNESCO in supporting Member States in EFA planning and implementation, an evidence-based examination at country level based on analysis of 20 country case studies in Africa, Asia, Latin America and the Middle East. EfC reviewed UNESCO's actions in (i) integrating EFA planning appropriately within wider educational and national development frameworks; (ii) its technical assistance and capacity building efforts in the follow-up to EFA planning; (iii) its national coordination actions in preparing and following up the EFA planning; (iv) its support of national, sub-regional and regional EFA forums and strategies; (v) its support of data collection, reporting and monitoring and evaluation of the implementation of EFA.

If you are operating in a partnership, each of the partner organisations should be described in a capability statement. If possible, you should try to stop this section becoming a monster – too long and detailed! Try to restrict past project or work summaries to five or six per partner. You can include longer lists and descriptions of relevant work in the appendices.

Roles and responsibilities

You will need to describe the precise roles and responsibilities of each partner in the consortium (if appropriate) and their relationship to each other. I find this is best done schematically if possible to keep the details quite succinct. For example, the draft ERPANET proposal included the diagram in Figure 10.3 summarising the roles of the network members.

Personnel

Key personnel in the project team will need to be named and you should include a brief biographical summary of each team member in the main body of the report. Full curriculum vitae are best put into the appendices unless the funder or client specifies a different approach. You should make the roles and responsibilities of each project team member clear, as in the following example.

Figure 10.3 Roles of the network partners in ERPANET (draft)

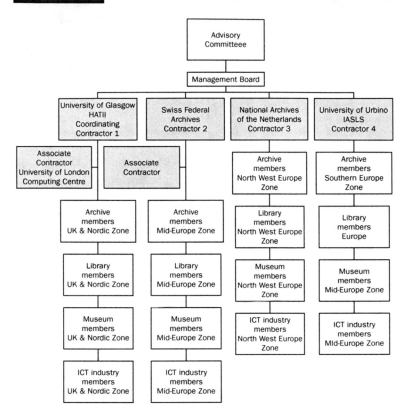

Example: Roles and responsibilities for a project team

Position	Name	Expertise and responsibilities
Project Director and Lead Consultant	Julie Carpenter, Director EfC	Julie Carpenter has wide experience of developing and managing evaluative, strategic and ground-clearing studies in the education and cultural heritage sectors, particularly in relation to the development and use of information and communications

Position	Name	Expertise and responsibilities
		technology (ICT) in delivering research support and access to collections and resources. She recently was the Lead Consultant for the ESRC on the evaluation of SOSIG and directed the evaluation of the impact of the Big Lottery Fund's ICT Content Programmes, with investments valued at £55 million disbursed among a very wide range of stakeholders. She also provides strategic advice to the National Maritime Museum on developing its services to social science and history researchers. Her specific responsibilities in this study will be managing the overall study, developing research and survey instruments, survey implementation.
Consultant	Nick Moore, Managing Partner, Acumen	Professor Nick Moore is a social scientist with a formal background in economics and policy studies. He was appointed as the first professor at Birmingham Polytechnic in 1987 and subsequently held professorial appointments at City University and the University of Brighton. He is a Research Fellow at Bristol University. In the late 1980s he established, at the Policy Studies Institute, Europe's largest research team focused on the social and policy issues that arise from the emergence of information-based societies. In 1998 he returned to Acumen, the company he first established in 1983, to pursue his research and consultancy interests.

Position	Name	Expertise and responsibilities
		His specific responsibilities will be working with the British Library on collection assessment and consultation with the social science community.
Research Support	Meg Goodman, Project Manager EfC	Meg Goodman has considerable experience of research practice and manages a number of EfC research and evaluation projects. She undertakes telephone interviews, assists in the facilitation of focus groups and arranges timetables, travel and appointments, as necessary. Her previous experience was in the voluntary charitable sector, where she worked on health and social policy analysis, research and information-provision.

Her responsibilities in this study will be research support and administration and routine reporting. |

Appendices

The funder may specify a range of financial and other documentation (such as annual accounts, a signed letter of commitment, certification from tax authorities, etc.) that they require to be in the appendices. In addition to your project team's curricula vitae and a possible long list of recent, relevant experience by your organisation and/or partners, you may consider including the following kinds of things:

- detailed technical specifications;
- examples of research instruments, such as past questionnaires;

- references from previous funding organisations or clients;
- detailed data from your preparatory research into, for instance, audience needs.

Checklist: Reviewing your proposal

1. Review the content of the proposal against the brief or instructions from the funders. Have all the required topics and issues been covered? Does it address all the points raised by the funder?

2. Review the structure and length of the proposal: is it too long and unwieldy? Can any more material be moved into the appendices? Does the structure match the requirements of the funder?

3. Edit the final draft proposal: are there inconsistencies in facts or information between the sections? Is there any duplication or repetition that is unnecessary? Can you further clarify and simplify the language? Have the different writing styles of the various contributors been made consistent?

4. Has your proposal been proofread by someone other than you?

5. Review the page layout and typography you have used. Is there a consistent style throughout and are you satisfied with it? Have you used appropriate sizes of font and typefaces to maximise clarity and readability? Are the margins and spacings wide enough? Are there page breaks in appropriate places? Are the pages numbered properly?

6. Have you written the summary and included a table of contents if necessary? Does it need a list of abbreviations and acronyms?

7. Have you, or someone else in authority, signed the proposal in the appropriate or required places?

Notes and references

1. Jane Fraser (1995) *Professional Proposal Writing*. Aldershot: Gower.
2. See the guidelines on submission by EPSS at: *http://cordis.europa.eu/documents/documentlibrary/2812EN.pdf*.
3. Adapted from Fraser, op. cit.
4. Ibid.

Index

Printed in the United Kingdom
by Lightning Source UK Ltd.
130190UK00001B/296/P